Introducing the OECD AI Capability Indicators

OECD
BETTER POLICIES FOR BETTER LIVES

This work is published under the responsibility of the Secretary-General of the OECD. The opinions expressed and arguments employed herein do not necessarily reflect the official views of the Member countries of the OECD.

This document, as well as any data and map included herein, are without prejudice to the status of or sovereignty over any territory, to the delimitation of international frontiers and boundaries and to the name of any territory, city or area.

The statistical data for Israel are supplied by and under the responsibility of the relevant Israeli authorities. The use of such data by the OECD is without prejudice to the status of the Golan Heights, East Jerusalem and Israeli settlements in the West Bank under the terms of international law.

Note by the Republic of Türkiye
The information in this document with reference to "Cyprus" relates to the southern part of the Island. There is no single authority representing both Turkish and Greek Cypriot people on the Island. Türkiye recognises the Turkish Republic of Northern Cyprus (TRNC). Until a lasting and equitable solution is found within the context of the United Nations, Türkiye shall preserve its position concerning the "Cyprus issue".

Note by all the European Union Member States of the OECD and the European Union
The Republic of Cyprus is recognised by all members of the United Nations with the exception of Türkiye. The information in this document relates to the area under the effective control of the Government of the Republic of Cyprus.

Please cite this publication as:
OECD (2025), *Introducing the OECD AI Capability Indicators*, OECD Publishing, Paris, https://doi.org/10.1787/be745f04-en.

ISBN 978-92-64-53190-1 (print)
ISBN 978-92-64-89309-2 (PDF)
ISBN 978-92-64-83602-0 (HTML)

Photo credits: Cover © LightField Studios/Shutterstock.com; © metamorworks/Shutterstock.com; © Rido/Shutterstock.com; © KlingSup/Shutterstock.com.

Corrigenda to OECD publications may be found at: https://www.oecd.org/en/publications/support/corrigenda.html.

Foreword

Far too little is understood about the advances of artificial intelligence (AI) and its implications throughout society. In the education sector, there is much discussion on what AI can do to change the delivery of education, but little is known about how AI is shifting the ground rules as to what students should learn to complement AI capabilities effectively. If public policy wishes to do more than adapting curricula and instructional system post-hoc to every new AI tool that is thrown into the market, it needs to take an active role to anticipate the evolution of AI capabilities.

This report outlines a methodology to do exactly that. This methodology provides a set of indicators along key dimensions of human capabilities that each describes the development of AI towards full human equivalence. These indicators describe: Language; Social interaction; Problem solving; Creativity; Metacognition and critical thinking; Knowledge, learning and memory; Vision; Manipulation; and Robotic intelligence. The indicators are presented in scales of five levels, where the most challenging capabilities for AI systems are found towards the top. Grounded in human psychology, this approach offers a structured and high-level perspective on AI development.

Linking AI capabilities to human capabilities allows policy makers to gauge AI's potential role in education. For example, to what extent can AI emulate the kinds of social capabilities that are key to the work of teachers, and thus where can AI substitute or complement different tasks of teachers? And what are the implications when AI capabilities increase to the next level?

The indicators will enable ministers to discuss the implications of AI for the future of education – from curriculum design to pedagogy. This will involve how to configure space, time, people, technology and relationships in education in order to create the kind of learning environment that will educate learners for their future, not our past.

Beyond education, the indicators also provide a framework to enable Ministers to discuss the implications of AI for other sectors: employment, civic participation, leisure activities, and everyday life. In all these areas, policy needs to be looking to the future, not to the past.

Andreas Schleicher,

OECD Director for Education and Skills

Acknowledgment

This publication was planned and developed by the OECD's Artificial Intelligence and Future of Skills project team – Stuart Elliott (Project lead), Abel Baret, Shivi Chandra, Marc Fuster-Rabella, Brianna Jesme, Margarita Kalamova, Aurelija Masiulytė, Sam Mitchell, Nóra Révai, Gianluca Risi, Mila Staneva and Chi Sum Tse.

This publication would not have been possible without the invaluable contributions of the renowned computer scientists and psychologists who are supporting the project.

First, we would like to express our gratitude to the experts who developed the first OECD AI Capability Indicators (in alphabetical order): Ana Teresa Antunes, Joana Brito, Regina de Brito Duarte, Kexin-Jiang Chen, Anthony G. Cohn, Henrique Correia da Fonseca, Haohua Dong, Nicholas C. Georgiou, Miguel Faria, António M. Fernandes, Robert B. Fisher, Kenneth D. Forbus, Giorgio Franceschelli, Jonathan Francis, Arthur C. Graesser, Yvette Graham, José Hernández-Orallo, Cherie Ho, Ryota Kanai, Patrick Kyllonen, Christian Lebiere, Inês Lobo, Christopher Lochhead, Rebecca Martin, Elena R. Messina, Mirco Musolesi, Jean Oh, Ana Paiva, Rui Prada, Rebecca Ramnauth, Swen Ribeiro, Brian Scassellati and Ana Vilaça Carrasco.

Second, we would like to thank the experts who provided reviews or advice on the development of the Indicators (in alphabetical order): Phillip L. Ackerman, John Anderson, Guillaume Avrin, Eva L. Baker, Chandra Bhagavatula, Oliver Bown, Adrien Doerig, Angelo Cangelosi, Lucy Cheke, Emmanuel Chemla, Henrik I. Christensen, Michael Cohen, Ernest Davis, Charles Fadel, Dan Gutfreund, David Hogg, Jonathan Gratch, Sam Johnson, Zeid Kootbally, Noémie Le Donné, Joel Leibo, Martha Lewis, Matthias Michel, Harold F. O'Neil, Britta Rüschoff, Ute Schmid, Eric Schwitzgebel, Lorrie Shephard, Tadahiro Taniguchi, Marko Tešić, David Traum, Michael Witbrock and Hiroshi Yamakawa.

We wish to thank our colleagues in the Centre for Educational Research and Innovation (CERI). Edmund Misson, Head of CERI, and Stéphan Vincent-Lancrin, Deputy Head of IMEP Division, provided oversight, direction and valuable advice during the process.

This project and its team have greatly benefited from the dedicated support, thoughtful leadership and guidance of Tia Loukkola, former Head of Division. Before her untimely passing, her vision and commitment were instrumental to the project's development and success. We remember her with deep gratitude and admiration, and her contributions will remain a lasting part of this work.

Colleagues within the Directorate for Education and Skills communications team and the Public Affairs and Communications Directorate contributed to both formatting and the preparation of the publication.

Our thanks are extended to Mark Foss, who made substantive and structural edits to the publication, ensuring coherent, comprehensible reading.

We are grateful for the encouragement and support of the CERI Governing Board in the development of the project.

This publication contributes to the OECD's Artificial Intelligence in Work, Innovation, Productivity and Skills (AI-WIPS) programme, which provides policy makers with new evidence and analysis to keep abreast of the fast-evolving changes in AI capabilities and diffusion, and their implications for the world of work. The programme aims to help ensure that adoption of AI in the world of work is effective, beneficial to all, people-centred and accepted by the population at large. AI-WIPS is supported by the German Federal Ministry of Labour and Social Affairs (BMAS) and will complement the work of the German AI Observatory in the ministry's Policy Lab Digital, Work & Society. For more information, visit https://oecd.ai/workinnovation-productivity-skills and https://denkfabrik-bmas.de/.

Table of contents

FIGURES

TABLES

BOXES

Executive Summary

With the launch of ChatGPT in November 2022, the potential impacts of artificial intelligence[1] (AI) on human activities began to capture the popular imagination. Yet while AI is progressing rapidly, public understanding of its implications is not keeping up. Much work remains to understand how AI could transform human activity.

This report describes the OECD's new AI Capability Indicators. The indicators have been developed to provide policy makers with an evidence-based framework to understand AI capabilities and compare them to human abilities. Developed over five years, the indicators draw on a large network of AI researchers, psychologists and other experts. The chapters of the companion technical report (OECD, 2025[1]) were written by 32 experts and reviewed by another 25 experts.

The nine indicators cover a range of human abilities that each describes the development of AI towards full human equivalence: Language; Social interaction; Problem solving; Creativity; Metacognition and critical thinking; Knowledge, learning and memory; Vision; Manipulation; and Robotic intelligence. The indicators are presented in scales of five levels, where the most challenging capabilities for AI systems are found towards the top. Each level includes a short description of the sorts of capabilities that AI systems at that level can perform accurately and consistently. The rating of current AI performance on each scale is linked to available evidence.

The indicators are published here in *beta* form with an invitation for feedback from two critical groups of stakeholders: AI researchers and policy makers. The AI evaluation work of researchers provides evidence for the indicators, while the ability to interpret and leverage insights from the scales is vital for informed policy. Feedback from other stakeholder groups is invited as well. The OECD will release the first full version of the indicators after feedback from our stakeholders and the development of a systematic updating protocol.

Conclusions

- The OECD is uniquely positioned to play a leading role in AI assessment as an intergovernmental organisation accountable to the public that can provide authoritative results to the global community that draw on its experience with comparative international skill assessments.
- The OECD's methodology leverages available evidence to produce AI Capability Indicators that both reflect the latest research findings and are understandable to a non-technical audience. These describe the progression of AI capabilities up to full human equivalence.

[1] The OECD defines a system as a machine-based system that, for explicit or implicit objectives, infers, from the input it receives, how to generate outputs such as predictions, content, recommendations, or decisions that can influence physical or virtual environments. Different AI systems vary in their levels of autonomy and adaptiveness after deployment." (OECD, 2024[2])

- The report introduces the nine AI Capability Indicators derived from human psychology and their development by the AI and Future of Skills team at the OECD and over 50 external experts.
- The indicators are illustrated through five-level scales that describe multiple dimensions and tasks AI systems must incorporate to progress towards human equivalence. Evidence supports each indicator's level and is used to describe the capabilities of current AI systems, which range between level 2 and level 3 across the indicators' scales.
- The indicators can be used to map AI progress towards the human abilities required at work. Mapping indicators to occupational and task requirements and the resulting "gap" analysis can be the starting point to analyse how particular occupations may evolve as AI becomes able to help or replace workers for some tasks. The indicators can be used to prompt values-based discussions about how the capabilities at each level on the scales should be deployed in occupations across the entire economy.
- The indicators can also be used to better understand AI's implication for education. They can provide a framework for identifying where AI systems could enable transformational change in education, helping to clarify which teaching tasks may be reshaped and which learning goals may need to evolve. While the indicators do not prescribe value-based decisions, they highlight areas where shifts in the delivery and purpose of education are technically feasible, informing future discussions on curriculum, teacher roles, and student competencies.

References

OECD (2025), *AI and the Future of Skills Volume 3: The OECD AI Capability Indicators*, OECD Publishing. [1]

OECD (2024), "Explanatory memorandum on the updated OECD definition of an AI system", *OECD Artificial Intelligence Papers*, No. 8, OECD Publishing, Paris, https://doi.org/10.1787/623da898-en. [2]

1 Overview of current AI capabilities

The AI and the Future of Skills (AIFS) project at the OECD's Centre for Educational Research and Innovation (CERI) presents a framework to systematically measure artificial intelligence (AI) and robotic capabilities and compare them to human skills. This chapter gives an overview of AI performance across each of the OECD's AI Capability Indicators. The first section introduces a comparative table and provides the information needed to understand it. The table indicates the current level of AI in each domain and describes the sorts of capabilities possessed by cutting-edge AI systems in November 2024. Below the table, a brief commentary explains the rationale for the OECD's expert group rating of AI systems at that level and the capabilities that would allow AI systems to progress to the next level.

Comparative table of current AI capabilities

Table 1.1 features an overview of the current capabilities of the most advanced artificial intelligence (AI) systems. The current level applied to AI systems in each domain is printed next to a description of the sort of capabilities AI systems possess at that level. Below the table, a commentary briefly describes why the OECD's expert group rated AI systems at that level and the capabilities that would allow AI systems to progress to the next level on the scale.

The OECD has developed five-level scales to communicate progression in AI capabilities in a manner understandable to those outside of the field. The scales aim to provide coverage for all types of AI systems. The current ratings include narrow symbolic AI systems, neuro-symbolic systems, large language models (LLMs), social agents and robotics systems at the cutting edge of given domains. At one end, level 1 reflects long-solved and uncontroversially trivial aspects of capabilities for current AI systems. At the other, level 5 AI systems can replicate all aspects of the corresponding human ability. The intermediate three levels show the development of different aspects of AI performance towards full human equivalence.

The OECD explains its approach to develop the scales in Chapter 2 and in more detail in the complementary technical report (OECD, 2025[1]). The ratings of AI systems reflect the state-of-the-art in November 2024.

To be ranked at a given level, an AI system must consistently and reliably possess most aspects of the capability described at that level. For example, our experts placed LLMs at the threshold between level 2 and level 3 on the Language scale. LLMs have many aspects of language capability described at level 3. However, they are held back by their inability to engage in well-formed analytical reasoning, a tendency to hallucinate incorrect information and an incapacity to learn dynamically. Nevertheless, as LLMs fulfil most of the other aspects of language capability at this level, they are rated at level 3.

A prominent failing of current AI systems – the persistent problem of hallucination in LLMs – appears in a variety of ways across the scales, both directly and indirectly. The Knowledge, learning and memory scale notes that hallucinations will be fixed at level 5, the Language scale also notes that critical thinking will appear at level 5, and the Metacognition and critical thinking scale notes that critical evaluation of knowledge will appear at level 3. This diversity across the scales highlights some different perspectives in anticipating the relative difficulty of fixing this challenge; this aspect of the scales may need to be harmonised in future versions. However, one important function of the scales is to remind the public that hallucination appears as one challenge among many: several challenges need to be solved for AI to reach human-level performance.

Readers will note that our experts have placed all current AI levels at levels 2 and 3, which is an indirect consequence of our approach to constructing the inaugural scales. The scales aim to communicate the major developments in each capability from the past towards a hypothetical future where AI can reproduce all human aspects of the capability. In each scale the level descriptors outline the major development steps in the domain. Those already achieved are at the lower levels, while those remaining are at the upper levels. Levels 4 and 5 generally describe aspects of capabilities that are still difficult for AI to perform consistently and reliably.

Many researchers in the field may not agree with our judgements about the state of the art in 2024 or the distribution of capabilities across the five-level scales. The OECD encourages AI researchers to contact the Organisation to aid our updating process and better align the scales to the most recent developments.

The level descriptions in this chapter are abbreviated; the full versions of each level and its accompanying scale can be found in Chapter 3.

Table 1.1. Overview of current AI capability levels

Domain	Level (from 1 to 5)	Capability description[2]
Language	**3**	AI systems at this level reliably understand and generate semantic meaning using multi-corpus knowledge. They show advanced logical and social reasoning ability and can process text, speech and images. They support a diverse range of languages and adapt through iterative learning techniques.
Social interaction	**2**	AI systems combine simple movements to express emotions and learn from interactions for future encounters. They recall events and adapt slightly based on experience, recognising basic signals and detecting emotions through tone and context. They also perceive individual distinctions and apply past experiences to recurring challenges.
Problem solving	**2**	AI systems integrate qualitative reasoning – such as spatial or temporal relationships – with quantitative analysis to address complex professional problems framed using conventional domain abstractions. They handle multiple qualitative states and transitions, predicting how systems may evolve or change over time.
Creativity	**3**	AI systems generate valuable outputs that deviate significantly from their training data and challenge traditional boundaries. They generalise skills to new tasks and integrate ideas across domains.
Metacognition and critical thinking	**2**	AI systems monitor their own understanding and adjust their approaches accordingly. They work with familiar information that may contain ambiguities, requiring measured confidence and informed guesses. They can handle partially incomplete information by discerning what they know and what they do not.
Knowledge, learning and memory	**3**	AI systems learn the semantics of information through distributed representations and generalise to novel situations. They can process massive datasets for context-sensitive understanding but lack real-time learning capabilities.
Vision	**3**	AI systems can handle some variation in target object appearance and lighting, performs multiple subtasks, and can cope with known variations in data and situations.
Manipulation	**2**	AI systems handle a variety of object shapes and moderately pliable materials, operating in controlled environments with low to moderate clutter. They navigate around small obstacles in open spaces, accommodate objects placed randomly within a defined region, and perform tasks without time constraints.
Robotic intelligence	**2**	Robotic systems operate in partially known, mostly static, semi-structured environments with some well-defined variability. They handle short-horizon, simple multi-function tasks that, while well defined, involve inherent uncertainty. They can engage in limited human interaction, such as minimal interfaces, and manage some unexpected outcomes within familiar task settings. They deal with little to no ethical issues.

[2] The descriptions in the comparison table are abbreviated versions of the relevant scale-level descriptions found in Chapter 3.

Commentary on current ratings

Language

As described above, today's most advanced LLMs, such as GPT4o (OpenAI, 2024a[2]) used by ChatGPT, are rated at the lower threshold of level 3. LLMs excel in accessing world knowledge, working across multiple languages and iterative learning through fine tuning and post-processing. The struggle of LLMs with robust reasoning due to their inability to engage in well-formed analytical reasoning and their tendency to hallucinate incorrect information continue to be a bottleneck for advancement.

Social interaction

GPT4o and equivalent LLMs are rated at level 2 on the Social interaction scale due to their strong social memory skills. However, they are not embodied, have no sense of identity and have limited social perception. Social robots such as Sony's AIBO are also level 2 systems but have a different set of capabilities. These systems are embodied and have basic perception and identity, but their problem-solving skills are much more basic than those of LLM systems.

Problem solving

Symbolic AI systems demonstrate superhuman capabilities in narrow domains like logistics planning and model checking and are therefore ranked as level 2 systems. While LLMs can fulfil some level 3 requirements, such as the capability to solve problems described in natural language, they are too brittle due to hallucinations. Our experts felt this was still true of early "reasoning" models such as the preview of GPTo1 (OpenAI, 2024b[3]) that became available in late 2024. Whether this is still true of more advanced "reasoning" models such as GPTo3 (OpenAI, 2025[4]) and DeepSeek R1 V3 (DeepSeek-AI, 2025[5]) is analysed in the full version of the OECD AI Capability Indicators.

Creativity

Current AI systems can create outputs that are valuable to humans, somewhat novel and occasionally surprising. One example of a level 3 system is Google's AlphaZero (Silver et al., 2017[6]), which produced efficient and surprising strategies for problems using a neuro-symbolic architecture. The reliance of LLMs on a probabilistic architecture and training data (i.e. previous human-generated content) means they are unable to generate outputs substantially distinct from existing human knowledge. However, these outputs are often useful and occasionally novel, which means LLMs are typical level 2 systems.

Metacognition and critical thinking

The most advanced LLMs typically perform at level 2 of the Metacognition and critical thinking scale. They can monitor their own understanding and adjust their approach to the problem at hand. However they struggle with integrating unfamiliar information or evaluating their own knowledge both required for level 3 systems. At the time of evaluation, agentic systems typically also performed at level 2, reflecting continuing limitations with AI's ability to self-monitor and adaptively regulate its own reasoning. Agentic systems released in 2025 will be reviewed in the next edition of the OECD's Capability Indicators.

Knowledge, learning and memory

LLMs and related forms of generative AI are the cutting-edge systems in this domain, reaching level 3 through capabilities such as generalising from stored knowledge. While efforts have been made with AI agents in this domain, none have shown capabilities required for level 4 such as incremental learning through interaction with the world or metacognitive awareness of knowledge gaps.

Vision

Cutting-edge AI vision systems are at level 3. Our experts have identified a small number of systems with limited level 4 capabilities. However, this performance is not yet reliable enough for any system to achieve that rating. Level 3 systems robustly handle a limited range of data types and can cope with modest variations in lighting, shape and appearance of target objects. Unlike level 4 systems, current AI vision systems are unable to improve performance based on self-feedback or cope with large variations of lighting and target objects.

Manipulation

Manipulation systems are rated at level 2. A typical state-of-the-art system is a robotic arm used in highly controlled manufacturing environments. In contrast level 3 systems can perform in moderately cluttered and dynamic environments with objects of variable shape, size and weight. Manipulation systems are still far off human equivalence. However, insofar as objects and environments can be standardised – such as in factories – these systems will still affect human jobs and skill demand will still be impacted.

Robotic intelligence

The most advanced robotic systems are autonomous delivery robots and industrial automation systems, which our experts ranked at level 2. These systems perform well in structured environments with pre-defined tasks. Robotic systems are currently unable to perform multi-step tasks or collaborate with humans reliably which would be required to reach level 3.

References

DeepSeek-AI (2025), "DeepSeek-R1: Incentivizing Reasoning Capability in LLMs via Reinforcement Learning", *arXiv*, Vol. 2501.12948, https://doi.org/10.48550/arXiv.2501.12948. [5]

OECD (2025), *AI and the Future of Skills Volume 3: The OECD AI Capability Indicators*, OECD Publishing. [1]

OpenAI (2025), *OpenAI o3 and o4-mini System Card*, 16 April, OpenAI, https://openai.com/index/o3-o4-mini-system-card. [4]

OpenAI (2024a), "GPT-4o System Card, OpenAI", *arXiv*, Vol. 2410.21276, https://arxiv.org/abs/2410.21276. [2]

OpenAI (2024b), "OpenAI o1 System Card, OpenAI", *arXiv*, Vol. 2412.16720, https://arxiv.org/abs/2412.16720. [3]

Silver, D. et al. (2017), "Mastering Chess and Shogi by Self-Play with a General Reinforcement Learning Algorithm", *arXiv*, Vol. 1712.01815, https://arxiv.org/abs/1712.01815. [6]

2 Constructing a framework to measure AI capabilities

The AI and Future of Skills (AIFS) project at the OECD's Centre for Educational Research and Innovation (CERI) presents a framework to systematically measure artificial intelligence (AI) and robotic capabilities and compare them to human skills. This chapter describes the OECD's methodology to develop the *beta* indicators presented in this volume. It shows how the indicators can provide clear and evidence-based insights to policy makers about AI developments and their implications for society, work and education. The OECD also argues that the indicators provide a principled and cautious framework to measure progress towards artificial general intelligence (AGI). To that end, it gives policy makers the needed tools to independently verify claims from technology leaders and researchers about AI progress.

AI has progressed beyond our understanding of its capabilities

Depending on the source, artificial intelligence (AI) is either set to save the world or destroy it. In a landscape dominated by hype and fear, clear, reliable and nuanced information about the true capabilities of AI remains strikingly absent. Even AI developers do not understand the current capacities of AI systems – or how rapidly they are advancing. As an independent and authoritative international body, the OECD is well positioned to fill this knowledge gap. Drawing on its experience of comparative assessment, extensive collaboration with leading computer scientists and engineers, and its international perspective, the OECD has developed a unique methodology to deliver rigorous, evidence-based and clear insights into the real-world performance of AI. This framework offers policy makers the clarity they urgently need to navigate an increasingly complex technological environment and craft informed, future-proof strategies.

With the launch of ChatGPT in 2022, AI and robotics are rapidly advancing, and policy makers worldwide recognise the need to assess their capability. The AI Act of the European Union (EUR-Lex, 2024[1]), for example, mandates regular monitoring. For their part, the OECD Council's AI Recommendation (OECD Legal Instruments, 2024[2]) and the 2025 Paris AI Summit (La Maison Élysée, 2025[3]) emphasise the importance of understanding AI's influence on the job market.

Despite this increased attention, a persistent gap remains: **no systematic framework comprehensively measures AI capabilities in a way that is both understandable and policy relevant.** To address this gap, the OECD has developed a framework for evaluating AI capabilities, introducing its *beta* AI Capability Indicators (see Figure 2.1 for an overview of their development process). The OECD's indicators are designed to be:

1. **Understandable** – communicating AI strengths and limitations in a straightforward manner.
2. **Policy relevant** – offering insights into AI's impact on education, employment and the economy.
3. **Comprehensive** – covering all critical aspects of AI capabilities.
4. **Responsive** – tracking AI progress over time through systematic updates.

Linking AI capabilities to human abilities allows policy makers to gauge AI's potential role in education, work and everyday life. Existing frameworks that characterise AI capabilities such as MLCommons (MLCommons, 2025[4]) and Stanford's AI Index (Maslej et al., 2025[5]) discuss capabilities purely in terms of benchmark performance without any comparison to human abilities. Taken in isolation, benchmark results are unclear to non-AI experts, and even to AI researchers it is unclear how results relate to AI systems' capacity to perform tasks in real world situations.

In a discussion of the limitations of current AI benchmarks, the authors of the 2025 AI Index report noted that "(t)o truly assess the capabilities of AI systems, more rigorous and comprehensive evaluations are needed" (Maslej et al., 2025[5]) The OECD's framework is unique in its effort to compare AI capabilities to the full range of human abilities used in the job market, recognising that in many cases adequate AI benchmarks for the advanced levels are still lacking. The indicators provide a conceptual framework for identifying or developing tests that can evaluate AI's capabilities systematically across the full range of human skill domains relevant to life and employment. Frameworks based in AI performance on benchmarks without a human baseline risk being quickly overtaken by rapid AI developments. An additional benefit of grounding a framework to evaluate AI capabilities in human abilities is they are relatively fixed over time. In other words, the framework will remain stable and informative amid rapid AI progress until it truly surpasses the full range of human performance.

Anthropic's AI Economic Index (Handa et al., 2025[6]) adopted a novel approach to analysing the impact of AI developments on the economy by linking Claude.ai's capabilities to some human tasks. This was performed by analysing millions of interactions between Claude large language models (LLMs) and users where tasks that could be linked to those found on the O*NET were performed. However, this approach was limited to analyses of chat-based interactions with LLMs. As such, it did not aim to compare AI performance to the full range of human abilities used in occupations. The OECD's own approach to leverage its AI Capability Indicators to analyse the impact of AI developments on occupations is described in Chapter 4 of this report.

Acknowledging the limitations of its current framework, the OECD presents these indicators in *beta* form, inviting collaboration with experts in AI and human psychology. The ratings of AI systems presented below were finalised in November 2024 and therefore reflect the state of the art at that time. Future refinements will strengthen the indicators as a precise and responsive tool for tracking AI developments.

This chapter introduces the motivation for the indicators and the methodology for constructing them (see Figure 2.1 for an overview of the indicators' development). It also acknowledges the limitations of the beta scales identified during our peer review process. A more detailed discussion of the methodology can be found in the technical volume released alongside this report (OECD, 2025[7]). The chapter ends with a discussion of the ways policy makers can use the indicators to help answer the questions arising from rapid AI development.

Chapter 2 presents all nine scales, the descriptors of performance at each level and the rating of state-of-the-art AI systems. Each indicator also includes a discussion of what is important to measure in each domain and the available evidence of AI performance.

Chapter 3 gives more specific examples of how researchers and policy makers can leverage the scales to provide evidence-based analysis of the impact of AI and its implications for the workforce and education systems.

Methodology: A novel and unique approach

From tasks to capabilities: A new approach to assessing AI

Understanding the impact of AI on society requires more than evaluating whether it can perform specific jobs or tasks. While task-based analyses have been central in labour economics, they often lack clarity and coherence when applied to AI; most human tasks involve multiple, interrelated capabilities.

In recent years, the economics literature has moved from occupation-based analyses of the impact of AI on work to analyses based on tasks This shifts recognises that occupations are based on collections of tasks that will likely be affected quite differently by any given AI technique or other technology. This task-based approach has been a major innovation in labour economics research (Autor, Levy and Murnane, 2023[8]).[3] However, it fails to provide a clear framework for describing developments in AI. First, task taxonomies are difficult to understand because there are thousands or tens of thousands of distinct work tasks in the modern economy; in contrast, there are a relatively small number of basic capabilities. Second, individual tasks typically demand multiple skills that may be affected quite differently by any given AI technique or other technology. Thus, they fail to provide a clear framework for communicating key advances or limitations in AI.

The OECD instead adopts a capability-based framework, shifting focus from fragmented tasks to core human abilities[4] such as reasoning, language, social interaction and psychomotor skills. Grounded in human psychology, this approach offers a structured and high-level perspective on AI development. To

[3] For a task-based approach to evaluating LLM's impact on occupations see (Eloundou et al., 2023[12]) or (Handa et al., 2025[6]).

[4] Throughout this report, we use the terms "capability" to refer to the basic types of things that AI can do and "ability" to refer to the basic types of things that humans can do.

show AI development across the full range of human abilities, the OECD has developed nine AI Capability Indicators shown in Figure 2.2.

Figure 2.1. The development of the OECD AI Capability Indicators

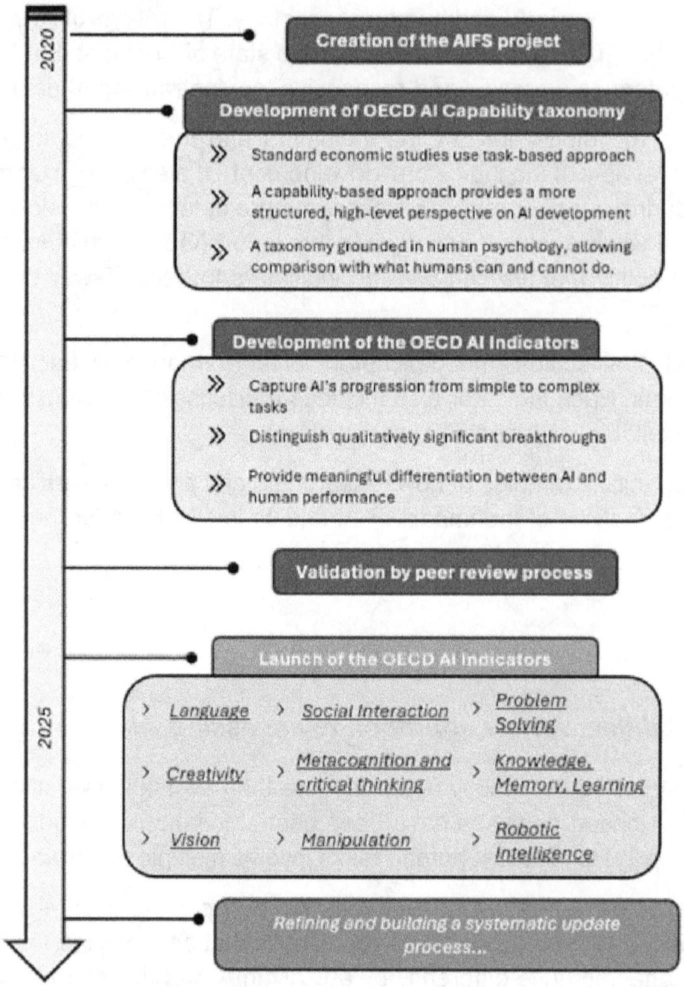

Figure 2.2. OECD AI Capability Indicators

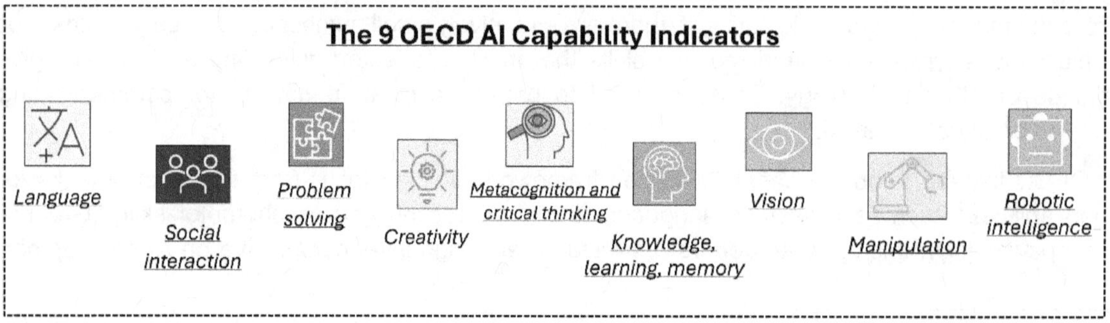

Constructing and developing the indicators

Building scales with five levels

The OECD collaborated with a core group of 30 computer scientists, psychologists and assessment experts to develop comprehensive indicators that **capture AI's progression from simple to complex tasks; distinguish qualitatively significant breakthroughs; and provide meaningful understanding of AI's capabilities compared to human abilities.**

The OECD created scales with five levels to represent the increasing difficulty of tasks for AI systems (see Figure 2.3). The scales aim to provide coverage for all types of AI and robotics systems. In the current version of the scales, narrow symbolic AI systems, neuro-symbolic systems, LLMs, social agents and robotics systems are all considered as they appear in the different AI subfields working on the different capabilities. In each scale, level 1 reflects solved AI challenges (e.g. Google Search's retrieval capabilities), while level 5 represents performance that simulates all aspects of the corresponding human abilities.

The OECD's primary motivation for developing five-level scales was to communicate progression in AI capabilities in a manner understandable to those outside of the field. Each scale generally includes several dimensions that reflect varying difficulties for AI. These levels are marked by clear qualitative differences, not just gradual improvements in performance. Each indicator identifies the current level of performance of AI systems on the five-level scale.

Ideally, each scale would be supported by formal tests with comparable results for both AI systems and humans, but such tests do not yet exist for many areas. Instead, the OECD draws on whatever evidence is available and uses expert judgement to fill in the gaps. The evidence may include formal tests but also competitions or analyses of the performance of individual AI systems. Expert input is also used to critically assess the relevance and interpretation of existing tests, ensuring that performance claims are well-grounded in evidence. Standardised human assessments such as the Programme for International Assessment and the Programme for the International Assessment of Adult Competencies have occasionally been used to evaluate AI. However, their primary value lies in inspiring the design of new AI tests that can better reflect the full range of human capabilities relevant to AI systems.

Future extensions of the scale may include aspects of AI capabilities that go beyond the scope of human abilities, which can be described as *qualitatively* superhuman aspects of AI performance. This contrasts with *quantitatively* superhuman performance. In the latter case, AI simply outperforms humans on speed, or accuracy or data coverage but is otherwise doing things that humans can also do. The concept of superhuman capabilities is not unique to AI. Historically, innovations like microscopes, calculators and power tools have enabled humans to perform tasks well beyond our natural limits. However, AI raises new questions about capabilities that require intelligent behaviour rather than just mechanical or computational advantage.

Figure 2.3. Overview of the five levels of AI

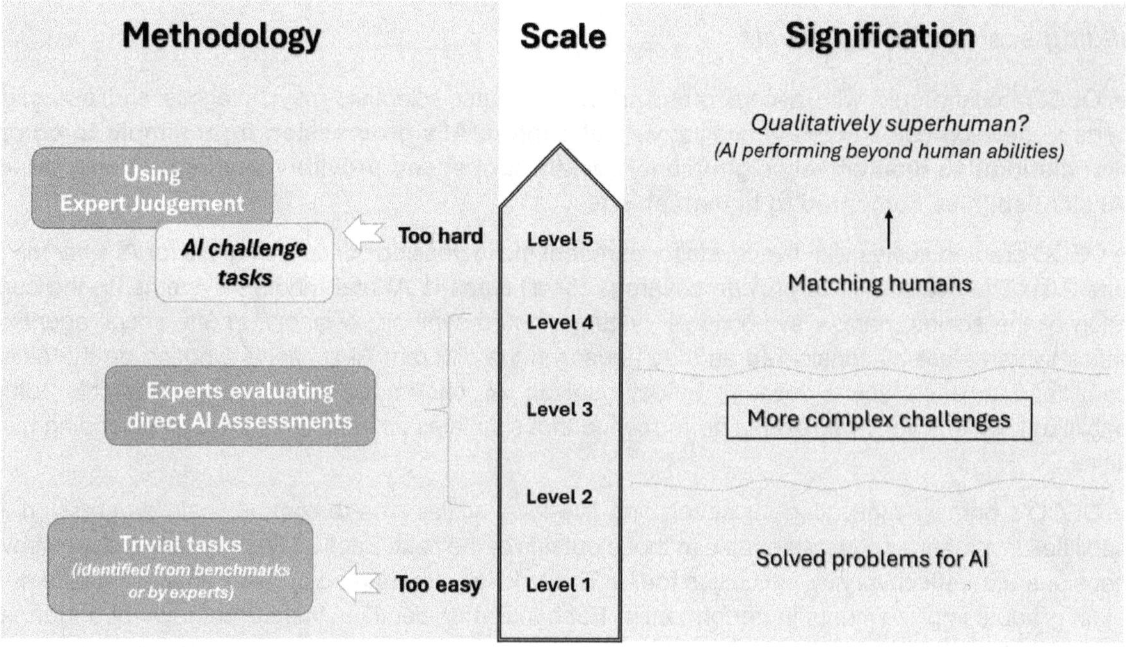

Validating the indicators

The process evolved over five years, culminating in a structured peer review in late 2024. The review comprised 25 researchers from the fields of AI, psychology and education, who were divided into two categories:

1. **Overall reviewers** – evaluating the comprehensiveness of the framework
2. **Domain-specific reviewers** – assessing individual scales within their areas of expertise.

Expert feedback has guided refinements, shaping the current *beta* version. Future iterations will integrate additional evidence, standardise measurement methodologies and enhance policy relevance. The OECD hopes for more feedback from AI researchers, psychologists, education specialists and economists to further refine the *beta* indicators.

Linking AI performance measures

The goal of linking AI performance measures to the scales is to identify the highest level on each scale where AI shows robust and reliable performance at a specific point in time. The scale levels are ordered by difficulty. Consequently, when AI is ranked at a given level it can simulate all aspects of the capability in a robust and reliable way up to that level. However, due to design constraints, any specific AI system may lack some aspects of the capability. The scales reflect the general state of the art, not specific system limitations.

Some scales highlight that lower-level capabilities in narrow applications may not be easily integrated into a system with generalised performance. The bottom levels reflect solved problems where AI is often quantitatively superhuman – performing tasks faster and more accurately than humans. Middle levels often have standard benchmark tests, while higher levels cover emerging or unevaluated aspects of the capabilities that still challenge current AI systems. Experts provided estimates for these higher levels, even in the absence of solid performance measures.

Limitations

A major challenge in evaluating AI lies in the uneven availability of measurement tools across different capabilities. While areas like language and vision benefit from decades of benchmarks, others – such as social interaction and creativity – lack formal assessments. In these cases, expert judgement helps fill the gaps.

Although a fully systematic AI assessment framework does not yet exist, this approach collects current evidence and highlights key areas for future development. The indicators are still in *beta* form, with plans for refinement through collaboration with researchers and experts.

The *beta* version of the AI Capability Indicators offers a valuable foundation for understanding what AI can and cannot do. However, advancing this framework will require deeper collaboration with a broader community of experts. Key next steps comprise:

- **Expanding coverage**: Include additional capabilities and indicators to capture a fuller picture of AI's range.
- **Refining structure**: Ensure consistency in benchmarks, account for multi-agent systems and manage overlapping capabilities.
- **Clarifying human performance baselines**: Provide greater consistency – or intentional differentiation – as needed to reflect meaningful contrasts in AI vs. human difficulty since scales vary in comparing AI to average or expert human performance.
- **Enabling dynamic updates**: Create a process for regular reviews and maintain a repository[5] of performance measures to stay current with rapid AI advances.

By aligning AI capabilities with core human abilities, the OECD indicators provide a transparent, policy-relevant tool for assessing AI's societal impact, especially in areas like work and education. While still evolving, this framework represents a key step towards a more systematic, evidence-based understanding of AI progress. A more detailed discussion of the methodology used to develop the indicators, along with its limitations can be found in the technical volume published alongside this report (OECD, 2025[7]).

Next steps

After the beta indicators have been suitably refined the OECD aims to pursue additional activities. This will ensure the indicators remain responsive to AI developments. They will also aim to help AI researchers design and implement valid and informative tests of AI capabilities.

1. Regular updates

The OECD will implement a cycle of regular updates. These will include monitoring improved AI results on existing AI benchmark tests that are linked to the scales. They will also monitor the scientific literature to identify new benchmark tests that should be linked to the scales. Finally, they will synthesise the results into statements about AI's current performance in relation to the scales. The updates will be vetted with

[5] The OECD is launching an online repository alongside this report to systematically collect evidence from benchmarks that test AI capabilities described in the indicators. At https://aicapabilityindicators.oecd.org AI researchers will be able to submit benchmarks and other forms of AI evaluation that evaluate any of the capabilities in our scales. The OECD will review submitted evaluations will be reviewed by the OECD and its expert group to judge their suitability for use in future updates of the scales.

the OECD's network of AI researchers and psychologists. The OECD plans to develop the updating methodology through the remainder of 2025, with the first update carried out at the beginning of 2026.

2. Anticipating AI breakthroughs

Thus far, the OECD has focused on developing descriptions of AI's current capabilities that have been demonstrated in the literature. To extend the indicators' potential usefulness in understanding AI's implications, the OECD will develop an approach to anticipating potential breakthroughs. To that end, it will invite expert groups to analyse key research plans in the field to describe the scope of potential breakthroughs in relation to the indicators. The goal is to analyse research related to capabilities that AI currently lacks to understand which capabilities may be poised for breakthroughs in performance. The OECD plans to carry out the initial effort to link the indicators to AI breakthroughs in 2026.

3. Expert survey

To complement expert judgements, the OECD will develop a formal periodic expert survey to review and provide input on key statements about AI's capabilities, modelled after the University of Chicago Economic Experts Panel (Clark Center for Global Markets, 2025[9]). This survey will provide regular updates on aspects of AI's capabilities that public benchmarks do not currently assess. Such a survey will provide early indications when new work is starting to focus on AI capabilities that have previously been too difficult for the field to address. The OECD plans to recruit experts for the panel during 2025, and then launch the panel in 2026. It will conduct monthly surveys following the Chicago model.

4. New benchmark tests and competitions

To provide more complete information about developing AI capabilities, the OECD will identify specific levels on the scales where benchmark tests and competitions are currently inadequate. These scale levels will reflect areas that should be monitored to identify when new AI capabilities are poised for substantial development. The long-term goal is to develop a new testing programme that can provide independent and authoritative benchmark test results for these missing levels of AI capabilities. In so doing, it would provide adequate information to the public about AI developments. The OECD plans to hold an initial workshop in 2026 to discuss candidate levels where new tests or competitions could be beneficial and identify available assessment approaches. This will lead to initial assessment development work in 2027.

The role of the AI Capability Indicators

The OECD's indicators offer policy makers an evidence-based tool to assess AI progress in terms understandable for a non-technical audience. This knowledge is particularly valuable for implementing major policy initiatives like the AI Act of the European Union and the OECD AI Recommendation.

Using the indicators to anticipate the impact of AI on education, work and society

As AI systems evolve, their growing capabilities raise new questions about when and how they should be trusted, deployed or constrained. The indicators help clarify which levels of AI performance may trigger ethical or safety concerns. These include decision making without accountability, or autonomy in high-stakes domains like warfare or health care.

Beyond ethics, the indicators offer a practical tool to analyse how AI capabilities align with the demands of human work. This makes it possible to identify occupations more exposed to automation and to anticipate broader economic impacts. While the indicators do not predict whether AI will replace human workers, they highlight where it could technically perform key tasks. This prompts deeper analysis of economic, regulatory or ethical barriers to adoption.

In education, the indicators provide insights into both the use of AI in teaching and the evolving skill sets students will need. As AI becomes able to perform more complex tasks, education systems must consider which abilities remain essential for humans – whether for practical, cognitive or intrinsic reasons – and how to prepare future generations to thrive alongside increasingly powerful AI systems.

A framework for defining and measuring artificial general intelligence

The OECD AI Capability Indicators offer a potential framework for defining and measuring artificial general intelligence (AGI), which is generally understood as AI that matches the full range of human cognitive and social abilities. While many believe AGI is still far off, some tech leaders and researchers warn of its imminent arrival and potential existential risks. In this context, the need for clear, evidence-based monitoring tools becomes more urgent.

Existing attempts to define superhuman AGI rely on characterisations of human abilities that are abstract and difficult to measure in practice. For example, Google DeepMind defined a superhuman AGI system as one that "outperforms 100% of humans" across all tasks (Morris et al., 2024[10]). In contrast, the OECD's AI Capability Indicators provide a framework to systematically compare AI developments with human performance across the range of human ability domains. In so doing, they provide meaningful descriptions of AI's capabilities and limitations that do not require policy makers to directly interpret the results of AI tests.

This is particularly important as AI capabilities will likely increase at different rates in different domains. The development of LLM capabilities has been described as a "jagged frontier" (Dell'Acqua et al., 2023[11]) because of relatively advanced capabilities in some domains (e.g. breadth of factual knowledge) and limited ones in others (e.g. formal reasoning). This is likely to continue with future AI advances up to and including hypothetical AGI systems. Being able to track the strengths and weaknesses across domains relevant to human abilities will be important to map the social, economic and political implications of AI advancements.

The indicators allow policy makers to track AI progress systematically, with level 5 performance across all scales representing a possible benchmark for human-level general intelligence. By capturing advanced AI capabilities such as creativity, reasoning and metacognition, the framework helps bridge the gap between public concern and technical reality. Where level 5 performance remains elusive, potential "AGI-level" risks can be weighed against empirical evidence rather than conjecture. This enables more grounded, forward-looking policy responses.

Supporting actors' engagement with the indicators

Over time, the OECD intends for these indicators to serve as a global reference point for governments, academic researchers and industry. Achieving that goal will involve several key strategies:

- **Usability and outreach:** Developing interactive formats and searchable databases so that a wide array of stakeholders can easily leverage the indicators.
- **Practical tools:** Providing both quantitative and qualitative resources (e.g. occupational vignettes) that illustrate how emerging AI capabilities will alter workplace and educational contexts.
- **Systematic tracking:** Collecting diverse use cases from policy, business and research communities to create an accessible knowledge base of real-world applications.
- **Continuous stakeholder involvement:** Engaging experts, practitioners and policy makers in the indicators' refinement, promoting broad adoption and collaborative improvement.

Ultimately, these strategies aim to ensure that the OECD AI Capability Indicators bridge the gap between technical assessments and actionable policy. By measuring AI capabilities comprehensively, governments and stakeholders can more accurately anticipate the benefits and risks of emerging AI technologies. This will allow them to take responsible, informed steps towards sustainable, innovation-driven growth (MLCommons, 2025[4]).

References

Autor, D., F. Levy and R. Murnane (2023), "The skill content of recent technological change: An empirical exploration", *The Quarterly Journal of Economics*, Vol. 118/4, pp. 1279-1333, https://academic.oup.com/qje/article/118/4/1279/1925105. [8]

Clark Center for Global Markets (2025), *Kent A. Clark Center for Global Markets*, https://www.kentclarkcenter.org/us-economic-experts-panel/. [9]

Dell'Acqua, F. et al. (2023), "Navigating the Jagged Technological Frontier: Field Experimental Evidence of the Effects of AI on Knowledge Worker Productivity and Quality", *Harvard Business School Working Paper*, No. 24-013, https://www.hbs.edu/ris/Publication%20Files/24-013_d9b45b68-9e74-42d6-a1c6-c72fb70c7282.pdf. [11]

Eloundou, T. et al. (2023), "GPTs are GPTs: An Early Look at the Labor Market Impact Potential of Large Language Models", *arXiv*, https://arxiv.org/abs/2303.10130. [12]

EUR-Lex (2024), *Regulation (EU) 2024/1689 of the European Parliament and of the Council of 13 June 2024*, EUR-Lex, https://eur-lex.europa.eu/eli/reg/2024/1689/oj/eng. [1]

Handa, K. et al. (2025), "Which Economic Tasks are Performed with AI? Evidence from Millions of Claude Conversations", *arXiv*, https://arxiv.org/abs/2503.04761. [6]

La Maison Élysée (2025), *Statement on Inclusive and Sustainable Artificial Intelligence for People and the Planet*, 11 February, La Maison Élysée, Paris, https://www.elysee.fr/en/emmanuel-macron/2025/02/11/statement-on-inclusive-and-sustainable-artificial-intelligence-for-people-and-the-planet. [3]

Maslej, N. et al. (2025), *Artificial Intelligence Index Report 2025*, https://arxiv.org/abs/2504.07139. [5]

MLCommons (2025), *Better AI for Everyone*, https://mlcommons.org/ (accessed on 27 May 2025). [4]

Morris, M. et al. (2024), *Levels of AGI for Operationalizing Progress on the Path to AGI*, DeepMind, https://deepmind.google/research/publications/66938. [10]

OECD (2025), *AI and the Future of Skills Volume 3: The OECD AI Capability Indicators*, OECD Publishing. [7]

OECD Legal Instruments (2024), *Recommendation of the Council on Artificial Intelligence*, OECD, Paris, https://legalinstruments.oecd.org/en/instruments/%20OECD-LEGAL-0449. [2]

3 OECD AI Capability Indicators

The AI and Future of Skills (AIFS) project at the OECD's Centre for Educational Research and Innovation (CERI) presents a framework to systematically measure artificial intelligence (AI) and robotic capabilities and compare them to human skills. This chapter presents the OECD's AI Capability Indicators, which currently provide descriptions of AI capability levels and comparison to human skills across nine domains: Language; Social interaction; Problem solving; Creativity; Metacognition and critical thinking; Knowledge, learning and memory; Vision; Manipulation; and Robotic Intelligence. The OECD is publishing these indicators in *beta* form to reflect its understanding that continued engagement with AI researchers and human psychologists will be needed to develop firmer consensus and ensure responsiveness to rapid developments in the AI field.

Language scale

Yvette Graham, Arthur Graesser and Swen Ribeiro

Language is an essential human ability that provides the foundation for many cognitive tasks. The extensive work in artificial intelligence (AI) related to language enables computers to understand, interpret and generate human language. This is reflected, for example, in the large language models (LLMs) that have recently become prominent. Because language is important for so many human activities, the limits of language performance can be difficult to define. Following the scope of applications addressed by AI researchers, the Language scale takes a broad approach to defining AI capability in language. It thus incorporates several critical aspects of the diverse range of tasks involving language.

What is important to measure?

The authors identified six critical dimensions to evaluate an AI system's overall language capability. The first of these relates to the meaning encoded in the words, grammar, semantics, discourse and style of the language itself. The second and third dimensions relate to other key characteristics of language use: its modality (verbal or text, understanding or generation) and the number of languages covered. The remaining three dimensions concern the range of potential language-related tasks of a language system: its ability to access knowledge, to reason about its knowledge and to learn. Each dimension has a progression as the level of the overall scale increases – from rudimentary to sophisticated AI language capabilities.

Available evidence

Thousands of tests assess AI's performance in language. The review sampled half of the roughly 40 types of tasks typically used to structure the field, including question-answering, translation and dialogue systems. Each area considered one or more major benchmarks or "shared tasks" that are jointly developed by researchers to measure performance, and track and stimulate progress. The current performance in these tasks often aligns with one of the levels of the scale. However, the specific level may change when shared tasks are made more difficult as AI performance improves. The scale indicates typical types of tasks that roughly align with each of the levels. The technical report provides notable examples of specific tests for each of the sampled types.

Current AI level

Today's most advanced LLMs, such as that used by ChatGPT, are roughly at level 3. LLMs excel in accessing world knowledge but struggle with reasoning, learning and handling subtle language nuances and/or communication physical modalities as they are pre-trained, non-adaptive models. Unlike generative AI systems that aspire to be general purpose systems for multiple tasks, non-generative AI systems rank lower. The latter need to be trained on a specific corpus of materials and optimised with machine-learning techniques on specific tasks. For example, Apple's Siri assistant is a low (level 2) AI system. It has significant weaknesses on the knowledge and reasoning dimensions, as well as weaker language and multilingual capabilities than ChatGPT.

Remaining challenges

Current challenges that constrain AI's language performance include the difficultly of incorporating structured knowledge and lack of advanced reasoning capabilities. These limit AI's ability to assess truth, integrate logic or perform domain-specific inference. Linguistic and cultural biases in benchmarks hinder equitable representation, particularly for underrepresented languages. Current systems also lack scalable, continuously evolving learning architectures.

Table 3.1. AI language scale

Performance level	Level description
5	Demonstrates nuanced language abilities, capturing style, tone and humour combined with real-time world knowledge and critical thinking in real-life environments. It can process or learn any language on the fly from small datasets. It evolves continuously through lifelong learning, adapting dynamically without the need for consolidating learning cycles. Typical tasks include automatic video description generation (i.e. video captioning) and structured reasoning tasks, which rely on critical thinking, real-time knowledge and the ability to process real-world multimodal inputs.
4	Appropriately interprets context in communication, leveraging web-scale world knowledge for complex subject analysis. It handles all modalities and supports a highly diverse set of languages, including a set of low resource languages. Continuous learning allows major version releases without significant architectural changes. Typical tasks include dialogue, which depend on contextual understanding, web-scale knowledge and processing diverse language inputs.
3	Reliably interprets and generates correct meanings with multi-corpus knowledge, demonstrating some forms of problem solving, logic and social reasoning. It processes most modalities effectively and can support a variety of languages, even with a modest volume of training data. Iterative learning involves fine tuning and post-processing to improve capabilities. Typical tasks include essay scoring and text classification, reflecting multi-corpus knowledge and advanced semantic and syntactic capabilities.
2	Produces grammatically correct language, supported by single-corpus knowledge and basic problem solving and analytics. It processes two different modalities in the most well-resourced languages. Model updates may involve major architectural changes with retraining required for improvements. Typical tasks include syntactic parsing.
1	Relies on keyword matching or highlighting for language interpretation and generation, with no world knowledge or reasoning capabilities. It processes text input only and is monolingual. Learning is limited to human-written rules, with no ability to adapt or evolve beyond initial programming. A typical task at this level would be keyword-based web search.

Social interaction scale

Brian Scassellati, António M. Fernandes, Ana Teresa Antunes, Rebecca Ramnauth, Nicholas C. Georgiou, Miguel Faria, Haohua Dong, Regina de Brito Duarte, Joana Brito, Henrique Correia da Fonseca, Ana Vilaça Carrasco, Inês Lobo, Rui Prada, Ana Paiva

Social intelligence refers to one's ability to perceive, interpret and appropriately respond to social cues in dynamic interpersonal contexts. Measuring AI's social intelligence presents distinct challenges because humans tend to believe AI systems are being socially responsive even when they are not. The Social interaction scale involves an integrated set of multiple capabilities, recognising that full human social interaction involves extended, embodied interaction over time with other distinct, embodied beings. As a result, defining the full range of complexity of the social interaction involves integrating aspects of language, problem solving and physical embodiment that appear in many of the other AI Capability Indicators.

What is important to measure?

To capture the full complexity of full human social interaction, the Social interaction scale comprises three dimensions that describe the difficulty of the social context: embodiment, social memory and identity. It is possible to have social interactions without a body, restricted to a short moment in time, and without a distinct identity. However, a full human level of social interaction involves extended, embodied interaction over time with other embodied individuals. These three dimensions describing the social context provide a conceptual foundation for four social skill dimensions: social communication, affective skills, social perception and social problem solving.

Available evidence

Relatively few benchmarks address the full complexity of social interaction. The review of available measures focused on examples of AI systems that illustrate current work at the different levels for each of the seven dimensions. It analyses several well-known AI systems with respect to all the dimensions on the scale to illustrate the way the scale can be used to describe the social level of performance for different AI systems.

Current AI level

ChatGPT 4o sits at level 2 on the OECD's Social interaction scale. While it has strong social memory skills, it is not embodied, has no sense of identity and has limited social perception skills.

Sony's AIBO social robot is also a level 2 social AI system. However, its strengths and weaknesses are distinct from LLM-type social agents. It is embodied, and has basic social perception and identity, but its skills in social problem solving are more limited than those of ChatGPT.

Remaining challenges

AI lacks theory of mind, making it unable to infer social intentions. Weak social perception and reasoning cause it to misinterpret cues and execute poorly timed interruptions. Its social memory is limited, leading to disjointed conversations, while poor adaptability to norms prevents it from learning unwritten social rules. In uncertain situations, rigid decision making replaces flexible judgement, making AI struggle with ambiguous social dilemmas. Deficient emotion self-regulation leaves it offering generic reassurances instead of adjusting to the emotional weight of a situation.

Table 3.2. AI social interaction scale

Performance level	Level description
5	The AI seamlessly integrates into any social environment, naturally embodying roles and adjusting in real time. It has unlimited, adaptive social memory and a fully aligned, context-aware identity. Communication is profound and nuanced, with deep emotional understanding. Social perception enables precise inference of group behaviour and intent. Social problem solving reaches mastery, allowing the AI to anticipate challenges and adapt solutions instantly for even the most complex social scenarios. AI at this level excels at complex tasks like describing scenes from another's perspective, learning new social norms or gauging distant social openness. It leverages unlimited adaptability, deep emotional comprehension and flawless contextual alignment.
4	The AI achieves highly natural social behaviour, adapting gestures to different scenarios and managing structured social memory. It maintains a clear role in groups, handles ambiguity and nuanced communication, and understands emotional intensity and its behavioural effects. Social perception allows for motive comprehension and group role recognition. Social problem solving becomes highly versatile, using social knowledge to resolve ambiguities and anticipate outcomes, which enables fluid navigation of complex social environments. AI at this level manages nuanced tasks, such as attracting a waiter's attention, determining student disengagement or deciding when to interrupt a group. It uses advanced capabilities like adapting gestures, understanding emotional intensity and interpreting motives.
3	The AI interprets body language, mimics group interactions and updates responses based on past experiences. It maintains a consistent yet evolving personality and can engage in basic emotional exchanges. The AI's social perception allows it to infer social intent and interpret behavioural cues. Social problem solving becomes more sophisticated, allowing it to evaluate and implement multiple solutions to complex social challenges, reflecting deeper awareness and adaptability in diverse contexts. AI can handle tasks like co-ordinating turn-taking at intersections or managing simple group dynamics, relying on its ability to interpret body language, infer intent and respond dynamically to moderately complex social scenarios.
2	The AI begins to adapt socially, combining simple movements to express emotions and learning from interactions for future encounters. It develops limited social memory, recalls events and adapts slightly based on experience. Communication improves with basic signal recognition, while it detects emotions through tone and context. Social perception includes simple individual distinctions, and social problem solving evolves to apply past experiences to recurring challenges, enabling basic flexibility. AI at this level can manage basic tasks like recognising individuals and applying past experiences to recurring problems, but it struggles with complex co-ordination tasks like navigating group interactions or assessing nuanced emotional states.
1	The AI performs simple, rigid social behaviours, relying on basic movements and emotional cues. It has fixed, unchanging memory and static identity, using pre-set, scripted responses for communication. Social perception is minimal, allowing it to detect presence through basic input. Social problem solving is limited to simple, predefined tasks, making the AI capable only of constrained and basic social interactions. AI at this level can detect the presence of others and solve simple static tasks. It cannot engage in tasks like attracting a waiter's attention or co-ordinating turn-taking due to limited adaptability and contextual understanding.

Problem-solving scale

Kenneth Forbus and Patrick Kyllonen

Problem solving involves integrating qualitative, quantitative and logical information through multi-step reasoning, including analysis, prediction, explanation and counterfactual thinking. Comparing AI and human problem solving is challenging because tacit knowledge and the interpretation of everyday, unstructured contexts play a crucial role in human expertise. However, such challenges are often omitted from human and AI tests of problem solving.

What is important to measure?

Four key dimensions characterise AI problem solving difficulty. The first two dimensions involve the types of solution required and the range of alternatives considered, which were important in distinguishing the difficulty of problem-solving tasks in the early stages of AI development. However, most of the remaining challenges in problem solving relate to the last two dimensions. These involve the complexity of professional or expert knowledge and the complexity of model formulation and interpretation. In particular, the hardest remaining challenges share requirements for common-sense and social reasoning to identify problems in everyday situations and to transform them into a structured form that allows progress towards a solution.

Available evidence

Several relevant tests exist on both the AI and human side. For each level of the scale, we have identified five to ten AI benchmarks; human assessments that could be adapted to become AI benchmarks; and example AI systems where they exist.

Current AI level

Level 2 AI symbolic systems like STRIPS/PDDL planners, Satisfiability solvers and model checkers demonstrate superhuman capacity in well-defined domains like logistics planning and model checking. LLMs can be used on problems expressed in natural language, a level 3 capability, but are brittle and more at level 1 in the kinds of problems they can handle. Similarly, socially interactive agents can solve problems requiring basic social reasoning. This makes them level 3 in terms of communication skills but Level 1 in terms of kinds of problems handled.

Remaining challenges

Challenges include automating qualitative reasoning, addressing gaps in commonsense and tacit knowledge, and overcoming AI systems' inflexibility in adapting to novel or open-ended scenarios. Social intelligence remains underdeveloped, with AI struggling to reason about relationships, ethics and nuanced psychological interactions. AI has made progress in mathematical reasoning. However, physical commonsense reasoning about objects through space remains a challenge and time tests of these capabilities continue to reveal gaps in generalisation and robustness.

Table 3.3. AI problem-solving scale

Performance level	Level description
5	AI systems at this aspirational level would solve complex, multidisciplinary problems across domains like science, law, education and medicine, integrating tacit, social and technical knowledge aspects. They would form long-term relationships, deeply understanding emotions and perspectives during live interactions. These systems would navigate ethical challenges, excel in conversational and persuasive tasks, resolve conflicts, detect nuanced issues like bullying and communicate professional knowledge effectively in accessible ways. Achieving this capability remains beyond current technological limits. An AI system at this level can identify and solve unstructured, real-world problems that involve social complexity; require solution approaches from multiple domains; and interact with other problems.
4	AI systems at this level are expected to solve everyday commonsense and some professional problems in fields like medicine, law and journalism. They engage users by building rapport, leveraging social, psychological and physical knowledge. These systems learn from past experiences, improving future performance and adaptability. They represent a step towards broader unstructured problem solving, offering capabilities that combine effective interaction, domain-specific reasoning and continuous self-improvement. AI systems at this level can interpret interactions in a complex social environment, identify problems that need to be solved and develop an approach for solving those problems.
3	AI systems at this level can handle problems described in everyday language, translating informal descriptions into structured models. They can incorporate social cognition and theory of mind reasoning, simulating human mental states and predicting intentions. They analyse interactions involving animate and non-animate dynamics, excelling in tasks like identifying emotions or intentions in conversations and making ethical decisions. These systems showcase advanced contextual understanding, allowing them to perform nuanced tasks such as moral reasoning, emotional identification and social interaction analysis. AI systems at this level can solve problems in areas like mathematics, the natural sciences, medicine or engineering, where the problem is described in everyday terms. These problems are like the questions on standardised human tests in these areas that specifically involve word problems. Other AI systems at this level can solve problems related to social and ethical reasoning where the problems are directly described.
2	AI systems at this level integrate qualitative reasoning, such as spatial or temporal relationships, with quantitative analysis to address complex challenges. These systems can envision multiple qualitative states and transitions, predicting how systems might evolve or change over time, enabling them to solve more dynamic and nuanced problems than those at level 1. AI systems at this level can solve problems in areas like mathematics, the natural sciences, medicine or engineering, where the problem is described using conventional domain abstractions.
1	AI systems at this level operate in structured domains, using precise, domain-specific terms like logical constraints, mathematical equations or simulations to solve problems. They analyse data for discrepancies, missing values or inconsistencies, and perform tasks such as planning and scheduling. In medicine, they diagnose straightforward issues based on structured data like interview responses or test results, staying within predefined parameters and narrow applications. AI systems at this level can solve structured problems in areas like mathematics, the natural sciences, medicine or engineering, where the problem is specified. These problems are like the questions on typical standardised human tests in these areas.

Creativity scale

Giorgio Franceschelli and Mirco Musolesi

Creativity is recognised as an important human ability, often linked to both problem solving and artistic expression. Creativity is often assumed to be exclusively human and outside the limits of AI, but it is important to understand AI's creative capabilities empirically. Given that human creativity has been defined in hundred or more different ways, it is already difficult to measure it uncontroversially in humans. In addition, AI systems typically lack the autonomy that is a key aspect of notable creativity in humans. Insights from well-known human creativity frameworks by Boden (2003[1]) and Rhodes (1961[2]) have been used to construct a Creativity scale for AI. However, machine creativity may ultimately require dimensions different than those used to describe human creativity.

What is important to measure?

The proposed scale evaluates AI creativity at the lower levels by the value, novelty, transformativity and surprise of their outputs. At higher levels on the scale, attention shifts at the AI system's intentionality, self-assessment and adaptability.

Available evidence

No comprehensive benchmarks exist for evaluating AI creativity. Recently, several domain-specific metrics and benchmarks have been proposed. However, they primarily focus on effectiveness and diversity, addressing only the lower scale. The initial work in developing the scale has identified a set of examples of current AI systems that illustrate the type of creativity they can produce.

Current AI level

Current AI systems can create products, which are valuable (level 1) to human users. These outputs can also be novel (level 2) and surprising (level 3), qualities that are apparent in recent foundational models and diffusion models. Indeed, novelty and surprise are also found in decision-making systems such as AlphaZero,[3] which produce unexpectedly efficient strategies for a wide variety of problems.

Remaining challenges

Given their probabilistic architecture and training data (which are a collection of pre-existing human artefacts), most generative AI systems (such as LLMs) struggle to produce surprising outputs. Given their reliance on human-generated text, LLMs also seem unable to produce outputs that transform (i.e. advance) human thought. Current AI systems are also unable to replicate higher-order human capabilities like intentionality, self-assessment and adaptability to shifting environments.

Implications

Until recently, creativity was once thought to be an exclusively human ability. Indeed, systematic evaluations of AI creativity are still lacking. Therefore, the authors recommend that policy makers support efforts to develop frameworks and benchmarks in this domain.

Policy makers should also focus on promoting human oversight of creative AI systems. They should also address intellectual property disputes, particularly with regard to outputs that draw from styles or products initially developed by human artists or other AI systems.

Table 3.4. AI creativity scale

Performance level	Level description
5	AI achieves intentionality, authenticity and full agency, creating transformative outputs on par with those of world-class human creators. It autonomously determines what and when to produce driven by its intrinsic goals, and possesses the ability to critique, reimagine and situate itself within a cultural context. Outputs transcend existing combinations, introducing entirely new aesthetics or paradigms, appreciated by humans or even other AI systems. Examples of tasks might include designing a new fashion style that dominates the fashion market; writing an international bestseller autobiographical book acclaimed by critics; or designing an innovative technology that disrupts existing markets and sets new industry standards.
4	AI incorporates process-oriented creativity, adapting its outputs to evolving domains. Through iterative and blind exploratory search, it refines results to ensure quality and appropriateness for the context. Demonstrating domain-relevant and creativity-relevant skills, it mirrors the creativity of the general population, balancing innovation with contextual relevance. Examples of tasks might include writing a speech for a special occasion. A speech for a wedding, for example, could select and link key events of the lives of newlyweds in a humorous, personal yet appropriate way; composing a letter for a newspaper reflecting on the mood of a nation after a sad event; or writing journal entries that thoughtfully recount the day's events.
3	AI generates outputs that are valuable, novel and surprising, deviating significantly from training data and expectations. It generalises skills to new tasks, integrates ideas across domains and produces solutions that challenge traditional boundaries. In this way, it fully satisfies creativity's three pillars: value, novelty and surprise. Examples of tasks might include winning videogames by devising unexpected strategies; participating in a political debate and successfully arguing a point; or composing an installation that integrates visual art, music and interactive elements to convey a complex narrative.
2	AI moves beyond imitation to create valuable, novel solutions. These outputs differ from those directly derived from training or programming. The system explores possibilities within task constraints, meeting foundational criteria for creativity: value and novelty. This aligns with inventions that are useful and non-obvious. Examples of tasks might include painting a portrait of a contemporary head of state in the style of Dutch masters; writing a short story that blends genres, such as science fiction and historical novels; or developing videogames with levels where the players explore automatically generated cities that follow topological rules, ensuring that each level is novel.
1	AI replicates human outputs or actions to solve non-trivial tasks effectively. Its results are valuable, i.e. typical and relevant, resembling human work but without true creative properties. This foundational stage reflects mimicry as a steppingstone towards creativity, akin to cover bands or copyists. Examples of tasks might include generating a variation of a culinary recipe by sensibly substituting an ingredient given a cookbook; drawing an object with modifications to a set of examples; or creating a simple piece of music that follows a specific meter and style.

Metacognition and critical thinking scale

José Hernández-Orallo and Kexin-Jiang Chen

Metacognition refers to a system's capability to evaluate its own reasoning, calibrate confidence and identify relevant information in complex tasks. Measuring this capability presents unique challenges. For both humans and AI systems, it is hard to distinguish between genuine metacognitive processes and heuristics. Existing evaluation frameworks often conflate task complexity with metacognitive demand, limiting their effectiveness. The authors use the research on metacognition and critical thinking in humans to develop a corresponding scale for AI.

What is important to measure?

The proposed model comprises three core dimensions: the need for critical thinking processes to assess the strategy and monitor progress when performing a cognitive task; the system's accurate assessment in how likely it is to know a specific fact or solve a particular problem; and the ability of the system to identify what information is given and what is needed to solve a particular problem. These dimensions form the foundation for evaluating AI's capability to self-monitor, adjust reasoning based on uncertainty and distinguish between essential and extraneous information. The model aims to capture both explicit reasoning strategies and implicit self-assessment mechanisms, addressing a key limitation in traditional AI benchmarks.

Available evidence

The scale was developed using a quantitative approach for task demand levels without referring to AI or humans in their description. It was prototyped with three benchmarks from BIG-bench (Srivastava et al., 2022[3]) that address the dimensions used in the model. The Evaluating Information Essentiality benchmark (Papers with Code, n.d.[4]) measures how well AI identifies required information for answering a question. The Known Unknowns benchmark evaluates AI's ability to estimate whether a specific fact is likely to be knowable. Finally, the VitaminC Fact Verification benchmark (Schuster, Fisch and Barzilay, 2021[5]) assesses AI's ability to reason about conflicting evidence. The approach estimated the metacognitive and critical thinking demands for each question in the benchmarks and compared current LLM performance to the estimated level. Additionally, generic benchmarks from the Holistic Evaluation of Language Models (Liang et al., 2022[6]) were used to contrast metacognitive performance with general task difficulty. This determined the sensitivity of the benchmark questions to metacognition and critical thinking.

Current AI level

State-of-the-art models such as GPT-3.5 and GPT-4 generally perform at levels 2-3 on the Metacognition and critical thinking scale. While they demonstrate basic confidence calibration and critical thinking, they struggle with more sophisticated metacognition and critical reasoning required for levels 4 and 5. Agentic systems typically perform below level 3, indicating significant limitations in AI's ability to self-monitor and adaptively regulate its own reasoning.

Remaining challenges

AI faces several obstacles in advancing metacognitive and critical thinking abilities. One major challenge is calibrating confidence in unfamiliar domains, leading to over- or under-confidence in responses. Poor benchmark refinement prevents accurate assessment of metacognitive skills, while the overlapping nature of cognitive processes makes it difficult to isolate metacognition from other reasoning functions.

Table 3.5. AI metacognition and critical thinking scale

Performance level	Level description
5	The task involves sophisticated metacognition and critical thinking, managing complex trade-offs between goals, resources and required skills. Long-term tasks may intersect with others, requiring decisions about delegation, self-improvement or task abandonment. Accurate self-assessment and the ability to adapt methodologies are critical for successfully navigating challenges at this level. Example: An assistant must find a file with a name referring to an eclipse or similar in the computer and send it to Jason by e-mail. The assistant needs to determine if it cannot find it, what level of similarity is appropriate and whether it can access the email system and send it.
4	The task requires high-level metacognition and critical thinking, including active regulation of thought processes. Subjects face complex and ambiguous problems in unfamiliar domains, requiring careful evaluation of knowledge and confidence calibration. Relevant information may be incomplete or unclear, necessitating substantial metacognitive effort to assess and apply effectively. Example: An assistant must perform some paperwork and needs to determine if it has all the required attachments or needs to ask some people.
3	The task demands significant metacognition and critical thinking, involving the analysis and synthesis of both familiar and unfamiliar concepts. Subjects must critically evaluate their knowledge, make educated judgements, and integrate complex or nuanced information. Identifying relevant details involves navigating subtle connections and implications, requiring deeper cognitive flexibility and strategic problem solving. Example: A robot reaches a door that has a kind of handle it has never seen before, and it must look for information about how to use it or try different options to understand how it works.
2	The task requires moderate metacognition and critical thinking, including monitoring understanding and adjusting approaches. The subject matter is partially familiar but contains ambiguities that demand measured confidence and informed guesses. Relevant information is incomplete, requiring metacognitive effort to discern and apply key details effectively. Example: An assistant must do the weekly shopping for a customer, and is given a shopping list, a preferred list of supermarkets and a limited budget. The assistant will identify and resolve trade-offs (quality vs. price), react to offers or unavailable products in a critical way (replacing them with similar ones), given the assistant's knowledge about the customer's preferences. The assistant will only ask the customer in case of doubt.
1	The tasks involve minimal metacognition and critical thinking, focusing on basic interpretation or recognition of information. The subject matter is familiar, straightforward or highly specialised, allowing for confident responses or quick recognition of limitations. Relevant information is simple to identify, with most details provided and requiring only minor filtering or basic logical connections. Example: A robot must cook a Vichyssoise for some lactose-intolerant guests and needs to tell the user how long it will take. The robot needs to determine whether it can adapt the recipe to a substitute of cream without lactose, obtain the ingredients and do all the cooking using tools in the kitchen.

Knowledge, learning and memory

Christian Lebiere

Knowledge, learning and memory encompass critical processes within cognitive systems, applicable to both human and artificial intelligence. The core concepts are interrelated: knowledge represents structured information, learning involves its acquisition, and memory ensures storage and retrieval. These processes are foundational to human cognition and underpin many other abilities. Simulating the full range of human abilities in this domain has been a critical goal of AI development for decades. The scale is based on models of knowledge, learning and memory in humans that describe the key aspects of human ability.

What is important to measure?

At the most basic level, it is important to identify whether an AI system is capable of the kinds of knowledge, learning and memory seen in humans. Cognitive science distinguishes between explicit declarative knowledge that can be easily articulated and communicated in contrast to implicit procedural knowledge that forms the basis for different skills. Humans acquire information from a range of sources, including direct experience, observation of others, and instruction from books or videos. This learning can be passive or guided actively in pursuit of some goal. The generalisation of experience can take place through processes that are more unconscious and statistical in character or that reflect more symbolic and logical analysis. Humans have a variety of memory systems, and their memories change in strength and availability over time. These various aspects of human knowledge, learning and memory have analogues in AI systems.

Available evidence

The performance of different AI systems is currently related to the scale by analysing their design to understand what knowledge, learning and memory functions they make possible: what kinds of information can be stored, retrieved and learnt. The authors also describe a set of quantitative measures that could be developed to complement the qualitative descriptions. They look at how efficiently memories can be stored and retrieved; how successfully a system can identify and retrieve memories that are potentially relevant in a specific context; what kinds of knowledge a system can learn and how accurately it can generalise them; how well a system can carry out active learning to support its goals; and the breadth of tasks that a system can use its knowledge to carry out.

Current AI level

Current AI predominantly operates within level 3, constrained by statically trained models, statistical generalisation and dependence on extensive datasets. LLMs and related forms of generative AI typify this level. Limited efforts have been made in constrained domains to develop agents that can acquire their own knowledge (level 4), and to integrate diverse forms of knowledge, learning and memory into general architectures (level 5).

Remaining challenges

Key challenges in knowledge, learning and memory include balancing different types of knowledge, such as "how-to" skills (like riding a bike) versus factual knowledge (like remembering dates) and integrating knowledge that operates automatically with processes that reason systematically. Another hurdle is creating systems that learn quickly and effectively, as well as ensuring these systems can adapt what they have learnt to entirely new, unfamiliar scenarios. Currently, it is difficult for AI systems to combine different memory types – like immediate recall, long-term storage, personal experiences and general facts – so they work together seamlessly.

Table 3.6. AI knowledge, learning and memory scale

Performance level	Level description
5	At this level, systems integrate diverse knowledge types, learning methods and memory systems for robust real-time adaptation and reasoning. They achieve human-like cognitive flexibility and efficiency, while addressing limitations like hallucinations. Future advancements may surpass human cognition by overcoming biases and limitations. AI at this level can perform tasks requiring open-ended cognitive flexibility, such as performing scientific research, making public policy decisions and arguing legal cases.
4	At this level, AI systems learn incrementally through interaction with the world and other agents. They incorporate metacognitive awareness to focus on knowledge gaps and balance exploration with exploitation. Expanding this paradigm to open-ended, dynamic domains remains a challenge. AI at this level can perform tasks that involve operating in unknown, uncertain or changing environments, such as performing household tasks, supporting the elderly or operating in an open-floor industrial setting.
3	At this level, systems learn the semantics of information using distributed representations to extract meaning and generalise to novel situations. Advanced algorithms process massive datasets for context-sensitive understanding. While more adaptable than earlier levels, these systems require extensive resources and lack real-time learning capabilities. AI at this level can perform tasks that involve generating content, such as writing stories, creating illustrations, summarising information and computer programming.
2	This level shifts to searching loosely organised information without rigid structuring. Statistical inference connects search terms with relevant results, enabling flexibility in handling natural language and other unstructured formats. However, it struggles to generalise effectively when faced with incomplete or missing data. AI at this level can perform tasks that involve information search, such as online shopping, news gathering, travel planning and researching product reviews.
1	This foundational level involves storing and retrieving structured information through precise computational methods. Knowledge is represented in formal formats like tables and rules, with logical queries enabling accurate retrieval. While efficient for structured data, this approach struggles with implicit or ill-defined knowledge and requires significant engineering effort. AI at this level can perform tasks that involve precise record keeping, such as financial accounting, computing statistics or managing schedules.

Vision scale

Robert B. Fisher, Anthony G. Cohn and Christopher Lochhead

Vision is a key component of human perception and provides critical input to most cognitive and physical tasks. Human vision can interpret visual scenes in their full complexity, with a wide range of visual conditions and environments. It can be used to understand a wide range of objects and scenes, both familiar and unfamiliar. The Vision scale reflects the extensive work in computer vision that has addressed hundreds of specific vision tasks in successful applications. At the same time, it highlights how the generality and flexibility of current AI vision systems fall short of full human visual ability. Computer vision encompasses a broad range of tasks, from object recognition to dynamic scene understanding and autonomous navigation.

What is important to measure?

To characterise the performance of specific computer vision applications, it is important to describe the breadth and variability of the objects or scenes they can interpret, along with their robustness to variation in the visual environment. Secondary dimensions included in the scale are the diversity of tasks performed and whether an AI system can learn through feedback. The authors identified a set of 32 different component visual capabilities that underlie the performance of different computer vision applications. These include capabilities related to detection, localisation, property description, motion analysis, geometric analysis, pattern recognition and visual learning.

Available evidence

The authors collected two types of evidence. First, 120 applications out of a database of more than 600 computer vision applications were sampled to analyse their performance according to the scale. The sample was selected to focus on applications with relatively robust performance for their selected task. Second, collected judgements about the performance level of the underlying set of 32 component visual capabilities were collected from three sources: the authors' review of the literature; a survey of the computer science community; and responses from ChatGPT 4o.

Current AI level

The sample of 120 applications showed half of the applications performing at level 2 but with a substantial number at levels 1 and 3. There were only three applications at level 4 and none at level 5. Similarly, evaluation of the 32 component capabilities found a third performing at level 2, a substantial number performing at levels 1 and 3, and a small number performing at level 4 or below level 1. These two sources provide converging evidence that level 3 is the highest level on the scales where there are AI systems showing robust performance.

Remaining challenges

The key challenges in computer vision progress include the difficulty of handling diverse, shifting real-world environments and the limited ability of current systems to reason and adapt in real time. For top-level performance, vision systems will need to evolve and learn continuously rather than relying solely on static models that typify the current state of the art.

Table 3.7. AI vision scale

Performance level	Level description
5	At this peak level, systems perform tasks with the same level of performance as human vision. These systems can handle all variations that a human might encounter, including changes in lighting, perspective, shape, appearance, position and scene, both expected and new. They improve performance based on self-feedback and demonstrate the full spectrum of human visual capabilities, such as finding objects, delineating boundaries, identifying objects at both general and specific levels, estimating their positions for manipulation and understanding object interactions. These systems can learn new properties, objects and behaviours while adapting to changes in the environment. Typical tasks include complex object recognition, dynamic tracking and real-time scene understanding across varied environments, such as autonomous vehicles interacting with dynamic traffic.
4	Level 4 systems can be applied to a wide range of data types and contents, including microscopy; red, green and blue (RGB); humans; mechanical parts; and natural scenes. They cope with significant variations in lighting, shape and appearance of target objects, making subtle discriminations between similar object classes. These systems can improve performance through feedback, whether from self-assessment or external sources. They can perform many different tasks, although not all that a human can do. Their performance is close to human level in the tasks they perform, and they can integrate various tasks so the output of one can feed into another. For example, a kitchen assistant robot might need to recognise shapes, locate objects, identify manipulation points, track motions and assess the quality of results. Typical tasks include complex manipulation and analysis in dynamic environments, such as robots performing diverse kitchen tasks, monitoring assembly lines or conducting intricate quality control in manufacturing.
3	Systems at this level can be applied to several types of data and data contents, such as microscopy, RGB and natural scenes. They can handle some variation in lighting and target object appearance. These systems can perform more than one subtask and cope with known variations in data and situations. They may offer human-like performance in some domains but not fully match human capability. For instance, a high-end autonomous vehicle vision system might integrate route, road, weather and vehicle movement information along with detecting vehicles, obstacles, pedestrians and tracking their movement. However, these systems may struggle with tasks beyond their specific domain. Typical tasks include autonomous vehicle navigation, facial recognition and environment mapping for robotic systems.
2	Level 2 systems can handle variations in lighting and sensor position relative to the scene, as well as some variation in the observed domain. These systems are more flexible than level 1, able to cope with variations in speed and timing of actions, and changes in the objects within the scene. They can perform highly specialised tasks in environments with some variability, such as lane following and obstacle detection in autonomous driving, or face detection and recognition in security systems. However, they remain specialised and limited to specific tasks, requiring carefully engineered conditions for optimal performance. Typical tasks include face detection, obstacle avoidance in controlled driving environments, and specialised visual inspections in manufacturing.
1	At level 1, systems perform tasks in highly controlled environments with minimal variation. These systems can execute only one task. They typically perform it nearly perfectly but only in a tightly constrained situation. Most industrial applications, such as manufacturing inspection or postcode recognition, would fall into this category. The visual system might work well within a fixed domain of scenes and objects but struggles with any variation in the environment or objects. These systems often lack flexibility and depend highly on stable conditions. Typical tasks include basic object recognition in fixed settings, barcode scanning and quality control in manufacturing environments with well-organised materials.

Manipulation scale

Elena R. Messina

Manipulation is one of the key human physical abilities. It involves the ability to interact with objects in the environment, which includes the physical movements themselves; the necessary perception, including tactile, visual or other sensors, to provide feedback; and cognition to plan and adjust the movements. Robotic manipulation enables a variety of tasks, ranging from basic pick-and-place operations to more sophisticated actions like handling deformable objects (e.g. folding laundry) or assembling objects in cluttered environments.

What is important to measure?

The difficulty of a manipulation task involves several factors. The task itself requires basic actions, which can involve different movements, such as grasping, fastening or in-hand manipulation. There are also the characteristics of the object being manipulated, the environment in which the task is taking place and constraints on how the task can be carried out, such as time requirements or clearances from other objects. These characteristics need to be described to gauge the difficulty of a specific manipulation task. In addition, the level of a robotic system's manipulation capability will also be determined by its level of generalisation across these different factors: the range of basic movements, object characteristics, types of environment/conditions and task constraints it can accommodate.

Available evidence

A limited number of physical manipulation benchmarks are available. Even fewer provide leaderboards comparing the performance of multiple systems over time. The author identified a set of 11 benchmark tasks that included tasks at one more of the lower levels on the scale. No benchmarks that comprehensively cover manipulation at levels 4 or 5 were identified.

Current AI level

Current state-of-the-art robotic systems for manipulation are at level 2. For example, the robotic arms used in manufacturing are proficient at performing specific, well-defined tasks in controlled environments but struggle when applied to more dynamic and unpredictable situations. Robots excel in many pick-and-place operations. However, they encounter difficulties when handling fragile or irregularly shaped objects in unstructured spaces or if objects or their locations have high variability.

Remaining challenges

The key bottlenecks in robotic manipulation progress include limitations in dexterity and adaptability, particularly when dealing with a wide range of object types or unpredictable environmental conditions. Additionally, systems often face challenges in real-time decision making and learning, which limits their ability to adapt to new situations on the fly. Furthermore, when both high levels of dexterity and advanced reasoning are required, current robots struggle to handle complex tasks effectively.

Table 3.8. AI manipulation scale

Performance level	Level description
5	Robots at this peak level match human abilities in manipulation tasks, efficiently operating in any environment – including extremely cluttered spaces. They handle objects of diverse shapes, sizes, materials and dynamics with exceptional adaptability, including reflective surfaces, slippery textures and flexible materials. They can reposition objects in-hand swiftly, place them into complex orientations and respond to dynamic changes. They can execute tasks with precision, efficiency, robustness and adaptability equivalent to a skilled human under strict time constraints. They collaborate seamlessly with humans, understanding their own limitations and refusing tasks beyond their abilities. Typical tasks include helping dress a person or search and rescue operations.
4	Robots function in environments with significant clutter and occlusions, distinguishing target items from non-target items swiftly. They can handle both rigid and non-rigid objects, including those with moving parts. They can execute tasks requiring specific orientations or placements with increased accuracy, navigating tight spaces or obscured locations with more precision. Force-based operations requiring moderate adaptation are possible. They can generalise to varying object properties and environmental conditions but may require human confirmation. These robots can complete tasks within stringent time constraints but do not match the efficiency of a human. Typical tasks include unloading a dishwasher, force-based surface manipulation and object assembly in cluttered or dynamic environments.
3	Robots adapt to moderately cluttered environments, selecting and manipulating target objects amid distractions. They can handle a broader range of object geometries and materials previously challenging, such as reflective or low-friction surfaces. While they can reorient objects or place them in moderately challenging positions, rapid in-hand repositioning may still be a hurdle. They can perform force-based operations with instructions but without major adaptation. They can work within moderate time constraints but may not maintain efficiency with tight deadlines unless in controlled conditions. Typical tasks include reorienting irregular objects, setting a table for a meal and handling delicate materials requiring force-based manipulation.
2	Robots can work in environments with low to moderate clutter. They can accommodate objects placed randomly within a certain region and can handle a variety of object shapes and some pliable materials, but elastic or slippery materials remain challenging. They can navigate around small obstacles, but intricate manipulations such as rotating an object to a precise angle or sliding it into a tight spot remain problematic. These robots can perform tasks in controlled conditions but struggle under rapid response or unexpected changes. Typical tasks include picking up toy blocks from a table and placing them in a storage container and material handling in controlled factory environments.
1	Robots are limited to simple pick-and-place tasks within well-organised environments. They manipulate rigid objects with basic shapes that are easy to grasp, using uniform materials presents minimal challenges for sensing or gripping. They operate best in spaces without external hindrances, following predefined paths with limited adaptability. Deviation from the expected environment typically causes operational failure. They work with wide margins of error and do not require precise positioning, focusing on gross movement. An example task would be moving boxes of cereal in a warehouse from pre-taught locations and inserting them in cases.

Robotic intelligence scale

Cherie Ho, Rebecca Martin, Jonathan Francis and Jean Oh

Humans can move around their environments and autonomously carry out a diverse range of tasks, driven by a set of higher-level goals. This ability to act as an autonomous agent in a natural environment involves the co-ordination of the full range of human abilities. This includes perception and physical movement but also language, social interaction and various forms of problem solving. Integrated *robotic* intelligence attempts to simulate this level of human autonomy, encompassing a range of tasks that require the seamless co-ordination of sensory, motor and cognitive systems, such as autonomous navigation, human-robot interaction and real-time decision making.

What is important to measure?

The scale for robotic intelligence comprises six dimensions. Four of these relate to the task itself: the complexity of the task; the level of abstraction in the task definition, which affects the level of problem solving necessary to figure out what to do; the complexity of the social interaction needed to carry out the task; and ethical issues, which implicitly provide a set of constraints affecting how the task can be carried out. The other two dimensions relate to the context for the task: the complexity of the environment; and the level of uncertainty involved in the environment and the way the agent interacts with the environment.

Available evidence

Few benchmarks are available to evaluate the level of integrated intelligence in current AI and robotic systems. However, the field hosts several challenges and competitions in different application areas, such as complex manufacturing, space exploration and human service. Evidence was collected by combining literature review with several workshops and interviews to construct a consensus view from current researchers.

Current AI level

Current state-of-the-art systems, such as autonomous delivery robots and industrial automation systems, perform roughly at level 2 on the scale. These systems perform well in structured environments with predefined tasks. However, they struggle with more complex, unpredictable scenarios that require adaptive decision making, creativity and social intelligence. For example, while robots can navigate pre-mapped environments, they encounter difficulties when tasked with interacting with humans or adapting to unforeseen changes in the environment.

Remaining challenges

Key challenges in robotic intelligence include limitations in adaptability, problem solving and ethical decision making. While robots can be programmed to perform specific tasks, their ability to adapt to dynamic conditions, collaborate with humans and make ethical decisions in real time remains underdeveloped. Additionally, uncertainty in real-world environments often leads to suboptimal performance, as robots may struggle to make decisions when faced with incomplete or contradictory information.

Implications

Ethically, integrated robotic systems must address concerns related to safety, fairness and accountability, especially in tasks involving human interaction or critical applications like health care and autonomous driving. Policy makers must prioritise developing standards and regulations that ensure transparency, fairness and safety in robot design and deployment. Investment in research focused on adaptive, ethical and socially responsible robotic intelligence will be essential for advancing these technologies.

Table 3.9. AI robotic intelligence scale

Performance level	Level description
5	At this peak level, robots perform multiple complex tasks in unstructured settings, with highly creative goal-setting capabilities. They can refine ill-defined task specifications. These robots can adapt to dynamic conditions, learn from their experiences and generalise across a wide range of tasks and environments. They demonstrate advanced reasoning capabilities, common-sense reasoning and highly skilled social intelligence. Robots at this level understand their limitations and can make ethical decisions, refusing to perform tasks that conflict with legal or moral guidelines. Typical tasks include home-assistance robots for people with disabilities, robots performing ethical decision making and high-performance autonomous driving in diverse and dynamic environments.
4	Robots at this level execute multiple tasks with varying degrees of complexity. They can adapt to dynamic conditions and adjust their behaviour based on changing environments. They understand their limitations and use feedback to make improvements. Tasks in this category involve long-horizon, complex objectives with contextual dependencies. While the robots can handle uncertainty and make decisions in uncertain environments, their solutions may not always be as efficient or effective as those found by humans. Typical tasks include cooking robots selecting ingredients based on availability, autonomous wheelchairs navigating obstacles and autonomous aerial navigation near airports.
3	Level 3 robots can execute medium-horizon, multi-step tasks that require some level of flexibility. They can work in environments with moderate variability and handle tasks that involve several loosely defined subtasks. These robots can collaborate with humans, adapt to moderate levels of uncertainty and can handle dynamic changes such as changes in lighting, weather or unknown object types. They can perform tasks with multiple solutions but may struggle with more unpredictable or dynamic environments. Typical tasks include hospital robots handling both transport and cleaning tasks, robots assisting with furniture assembly and robot cinematographers autonomously filming based on learnt preferences.
2	Robots in this category execute predefined tasks in semi-structured environments with some variability. They handle low to moderate uncertainty, such as changes in object placement or the environment's layout. Tasks typically have well-defined success metrics and robots operate under minimal human interaction. They can execute simple, multi-functional tasks but are limited by their inability to handle more complex or unforeseen changes. Typical tasks include medical transport robots, material-handling robots in factories and agricultural robots for fruit picking.
1	Level 1 robots perform simple, repetitive tasks within highly structured and controlled environments. They work in static, deterministic settings where the environment is fully known and predictable. These robots follow pre-specified instructions without the ability to make adaptive decisions or handle unforeseen circumstances. They do not interact with humans and typically cannot handle even small changes to their environment. Typical tasks include basic automated assembly in factories, robotic vacuum cleaners and object sorting systems in logistics operations.

References

Boden, M. (2003), *The Creative Mind: Myths and Mechanisms*, Routledge, Milton Park, Abingdon-on-Thames. [1]

Liang, P. et al. (2022), "Holistic evaluation of language models", *arXiv*, Vol. 2211.09110, https://arxiv.org/abs/2211.09110. [6]

Papers with Code (n.d.), "Evaluating Information essentiality on BIG-bench", *BIG-bench Benchmark*, (database), https://paperswithcode.com/sota/evaluating-information-essentiality-on-big (accessed on 15 May 2025). [4]

Rhodes, M. (1961), "An analysis of creativity", *The Phi Delta Kappan*, Vol. 42/7, pp. 305-310, https://www.jstor.org/stable/i20342591. [2]

Schuster, T., A. Fisch and R. Barzilay (2021), "Get your vitamin C! Robust fact verification with contrastive evidence", *arXiv*, Vol. 2103.08541, https://doi.org/10.48550/arXiv.2103.08541. [5]

Srivastava, A. et al. (2022), "Beyond the imitation game: Quantifying and extrapolating the capabilities of language models", *arXiv*, Vol. 2206.04615, https://doi.org/10.48550/arXiv.2206.04615. [3]

4 Policy use cases for the AI Capability Indicators

The AI and the Future of Skills (AIFS) project at the OECD's Centre for Educational Research and Innovation (CERI) presents a framework to systematically measure artificial intelligence (AI) and robotic capabilities and compare them to human skills. In this chapter, AIFS discusses possible ways policy makers could draw on the OECD's AI Capability Indicators to model implications of AI developments in various domains. The first section outlines, an approach to leverage the indicators to estimate how AI will transform occupational demand. In the second section, the OECD presents how education policy makers can use the indicators to inform discussions about the transformation of teacher roles in education and how learning goals may need to shift to account for changing occupational demand.

Artificial intelligence (AI) is progressing rapidly, but not all advances will lead to major societal and economic change. The OECD AI Capability Indicators help identify where AI might have transformational impacts. While the indicators are too broad for evaluating specific AI applications, they are well suited to spotting larger shifts in how jobs and learning could evolve.

Because the indicators are new, the OECD has not yet applied them systematically. This chapter outlines how these indicators can be used to map AI progress towards human abilities required at work. It also explores how this mapping can signal possible transformations at work and in education systems, which can guide future policy discussions.

Mapping the indicators to occupational demand for human abilities

To assess how AI might lead to transformational change in the economy and society, the first step is to understand which occupations – and which component tasks of these occupations – require abilities that AI may soon be able to perform. This analysis begins by linking the OECD AI Capability Indicators to descriptions of occupations and their component tasks to derive capability requirements.

The AI Capability Indicators can be directly linked to the ability and skill requirements of different real-world jobs by comparing the level descriptions of the nine indicators to the job descriptions. This can be done in two ways: by looking at entire occupations with all their characteristics, or by focusing more narrowly on specific tasks within those occupations. The goal is to determine the capability level needed to carry out a job or task effectively along each of the AI Capability Indicators.

This work can be done using the US-based O*NET system because it is one of the most extensive datasets worldwide of occupational characteristics. O*NET includes data for about 900 occupations and its taxonomy has been adopted in part or compared to the occupational taxonomies used by many other countries. O*NET and the other occupational databases directly modelled on it comprise a set of occupational characteristics – including detailed tasks, work environment and required human abilities – that can be directly compared to the AI Capability Indicators.

This section attempts to illustrate the approach using the example of the teaching profession. As illustrated in Figure 4.1, a substantive part a teacher's job requires language, social interaction and problem-solving capabilities at some of the highest levels. This becomes particularly evident when the demands of a specific teacher's task are considered. The O*NET task "Adapting teaching methods and instructional materials to meet students' varying needs and interests" draws on a range of capabilities described at levels 4 or 5 of the AI Capability Indicators in language, problem solving and social interaction. Thus, teachers must leverage nuanced language abilities (language and social interaction, level 5) to communicate instructions clearly and tailor feedback to learners with different skill levels, cultural backgrounds and learning styles. They also engage in problem solving by interpreting interactions within a complex social environment, identifying individual or group-level barriers to understanding and developing targeted approaches to overcome them (problem solving, level 4). Additionally, teachers build rapport, handle ambiguity and respond to emotional cues, all while nurturing a supportive atmosphere that helps maintain engagement and motivation among diverse learners (social interaction, level 5). These early judgements are still tentative and would need to be refined through further validation and expert review.

Figure 4.1. Mapping the AI Capability Indicators of language, problem solving and social interaction to the capability requirements of teachers' tasks

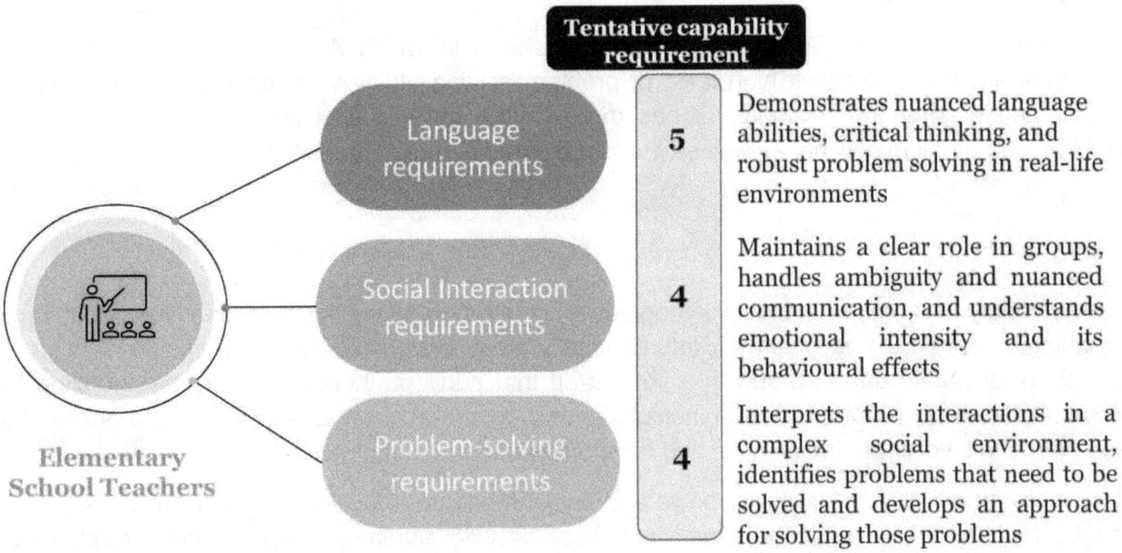

This type of analysis can be scaled up using a multi-step process:

- A survey of job experts can provide judgements of the level of capabilities required for carrying out occupations and occupational tasks from a representative sample.
- These judgements can be extended to cover all occupations and the tens of thousands of tasks included in the O*NET and European Skills, Competences, Qualifications and Occupations (ESCO), using AI-based techniques and statistical inference.

Once occupations and component tasks have been linked to the required level of capabilities on the AI Capability Indicators, the gap between AI's current capabilities and those required by a specific occupation or task can be calculated. These estimates can then be used to identify occupations and tasks that AI can perform at different levels of AI capabilities.

It will be easiest to identify occupations or tasks where AI possesses all required capabilities, allowing full automation. However, it will also be possible to use these analyses to identify occupations or tasks where AI possesses only some of the required capabilities. This would point towards potential human-AI collaboration with workers who have the complementary abilities that AI lacks. Such analyses can be used to create summary metrics showing how different profiles of AI progress on the indicators could affect different occupations and larger economic implications.

Mapping the AI Capability Indicators to occupational and task requirements can serve as a starting point for an in-depth analysis of how particular tasks within occupations may evolve with current and improved AI capabilities. Such an analysis will involve a structured discussion with stakeholders from the concerned occupation(s) to understand:

- whether the society wants AI to ever carry out a particular task
- whether AI systems already exist or are in the pipeline that can carry out the task
- what adjustments would be needed for humans to work along with AI systems.

The result will be transformed task scenarios – vignettes that are vetted by the industry itself, education and training providers, and AI experts. The vignettes can illustrate the way the teacher roles and certain other adult roles might change. This methodology could also be applied to capability profiles across different countries and at a subnational level. This will allow policy makers to identify geographies that are more or less likely to be exposed to AI and guide appropriate policy responses. A more detailed discussion of the OECD's approach can be found in Chapter 14 of the technical volume (OECD, 2025[1]) accompanying this report.

To illustrate the vignettes, Box 4.1 describes a scenario in which AI is at the midpoint on the AI Problem-solving scale. It has a high level of problem solving ability with respect to natural sciences, medicine and engineering. However, it has more limited abilities with respect to social and ethical reasoning, and problem solving, as well as moderate sensory motor capabilities.

Box 4.1. Vignette of AI at mid-level of the Problem-solving scale supporting pandemic response

In a blisteringly hot summer, a highly contagious mosquito-borne infectious disease breaks out, rapidly spreading to major cities nationally and internationally. An AI system has **identified** the problem through analysis of disparate datasets and **recommended** that public authorities declare the infection as a pandemic. Medical centres, research institutions and government organisations **start** a collaborative programme to investigate the disease and develop a cure and a vaccine.

AI systems continue to **track** online news and social media to **model** how the disease spreads and which symptoms it involves before more centralised data collection can begin. This information helps systems **detect** promising prevention and containment measures for public authorities to **adopt** and **implement**, and to begin considering effective treatments.

AI systems **design** and **execute** experiments **co-ordinating** dozens of robotic molecular biology labs to analyse samples and data gathered around the world – in real time. Before this event, biomedical literature has informed the AI systems and characterised an enormous diversity of biomedical research data. Using this knowledge, AI can **hypothesise** pathways where the virus might be interfering.

After prioritising the hypotheses, based on the known literature, human teams **implement** targeted experiments in mice. Working with the results, an AI system **discovers** an interesting link to a rare neurological condition and **proposes** a viable treatment.

AI helps governments globally to **manage** their stocks of medical material to ensure a fair and efficient distribution in response to the disease. Furthermore, AI-accelerated discovery is the key to **identify** the novel mechanism of viral action and **design** an effective vaccine. Within days, thousands of doses are **produced** and **distributed**; the disease is under control and those affected are in remission.

Source: Adapted from (Gil and Selman, 2019[2]).

In this vignette, **AI systems:**

- show strong capabilities in data and information retrieval, monitoring, analysis and interpretation, which are linked to their problem identification capacity and related research and development efforts.
- are able to identify, support and design solutions, in both the policy and health-care domains.
- can work with complex systems relying on scientific knowledge and the analysis of novel data. They work effectively with models in areas spanning human biology and broader ecosystem dynamics – including social and human-nature interactions – demonstrating the capacity of reasoning from evidence.

The **human role**, by contrast, focuses on:

- directing public and private efforts towards containing and eventually solving the crisis once the disease is discovered.

- ensuring that AI's experimental research protocols are administered and that vaccines are distributed effectively once developed and produced by AI and robots. A range of physical skills are required, notably manual and visual skills for various manipulation activities.
- employing social skills and ethical reasoning in crisis management and co-operation activities.

Transformational change in education

Building on the indicators and the occupational analysis above, a new framework emerges for examining the potential for transformational change in education (Figure 4.2). This example focuses on the education sector given its relevance to an education policy audience but could in principle be extended to any occupation or economic sector. This framework can inform decisions about both the purpose and delivery of education. It can guide discussion of how educational practices might evolve if AI capabilities surpass human performance in certain teaching tasks. It can also handle key questions about which learning objectives and curricular content may stay the same, need removal or revision, or which should be newly introduced – depending on current or future AI capabilities.

Figure 4.2. A framework for analysing implications of increasing AI capabilities in education

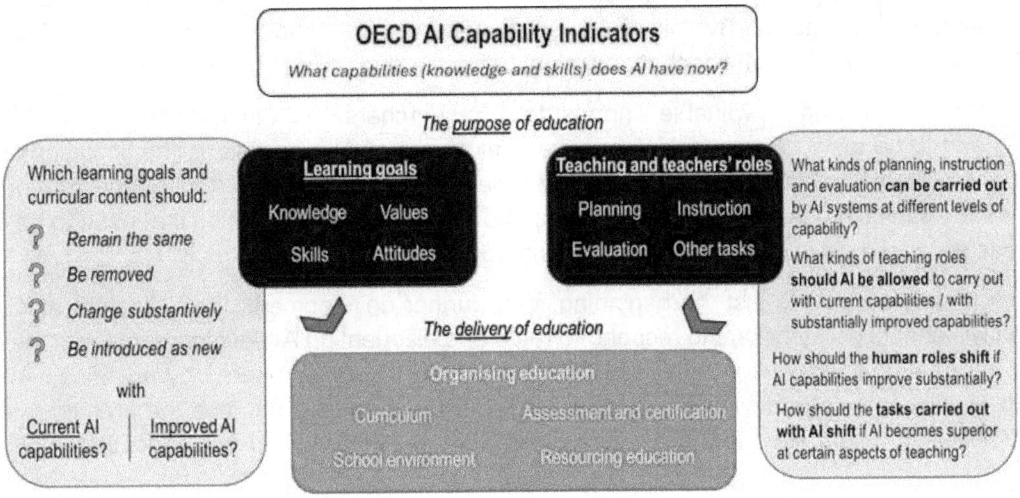

Two key types of potential transformation in education stand out.

First, if AI can perform a substantial portion of teachers' tasks, it could possibly transform education delivery. For example, if AI can reliably deliver instruction or provide feedback, the traditional role of teachers may shift towards mentoring, motivating or handling complex interpersonal dynamics. Such a development could redefine how teaching is delivered, sparking a transformation in classroom dynamics, teacher-student interactions and the overall learning experience.

Second, student learning goals are related to the kinds of tasks that society expects students to perform as adults at work and in their community and in everyday life. If AI can now perform many of these tasks, education systems may need to reconsider what students should be learning. These potential implications are already apparent in the ability of AI to outperform students in many assessments used in education, such as the OECD's Programme for International Student Assessment survey of the competences of 15-year-olds. As a result, some current goals may lose relevance, while others – like creativity or ethical judgement – may become more important.

Of course, these changes are not just technical. Societal values will shape whether and how the role of teachers in certain tasks is reduced or revise what students are expected to learn. The AI Capability Indicators and the occupational analysis above do not offer answers to these value questions, but they can highlight areas where major change is technically feasible and perhaps likely.

The OECD will explore these possibilities in greater detail through scenario-based analyses of teaching roles and student expectations. The resulting vignettes will guide the discussion of potential transformation in learning goals and curricular content. Chapter 14 of the technical volume (OECD, 2025[1]) accompanying this report provides a more detailed discussion of how education policy makers can leverage the OECD's AI Capability Indicators.

Conclusion

The AI Capability Indicators in this report offer a simple but powerful tool to assess how AI progress aligns with human abilities. The indicators are informed by evidence from AI evaluations and expert opinion. By describing AI capabilities linked to human abilities the indicators are understandable to a non-technical audience. They thus provide a clear framework for anticipating the impact of AI progression across a range of domains relevant to work and education. This comparison to human abilities also provides a clear measure of AI's progress towards artificial general intelligence and will remain stable amid rapid developments in AI capability. By linking AI performance to real-world work demands and educational goals, they help us see where major changes might happen – and where human roles will remain essential.

The indicators also provide a valuable signpost to AI researchers. They indicate the sorts of capabilities that will need to be tested to provide informative evaluations of AI progress as the limitations of current approaches to benchmarks become increasingly salient. They also provide a mechanism through which policy makers can communicate to AI researchers about the sorts of capabilities that need to be evaluated to address societal, political and ethical concerns around AI development.

The work presented here is just the beginning. With further development, the indicators and derivative analyses will enable policymakers to respond to rapid and disorienting AI developments with the clear and concise information they need to capitalise on the huge opportunities offered by advanced AI systems. The OECD will continue to develop and update the indicators so they become the premier international source for trusted information about AI capabilities and their implications for education, work and civil society.

References

Gil, Y. and B. Selman (2019), "A 20-year community roadmap for artificial intelligence research in the US", *arXiv*, Vol. 1908.02624, https://arxiv.org/abs/1908.02624. [2]

OECD (2025), *AI and the Future of Skills Volume 3: The OECD AI Capability Indicators*, OECD Publishing. [1]

www.ingramcontent.com/pod-product-compliance
Lightning Source LLC
LaVergne TN
LVHW060456061126
851857LV00016B/1845
* 9 7 8 9 2 6 4 5 3 1 9 0 1 *